**Housing and Housing Policy
in the U.S. and the U.K.**

Housing and Housing Policy in the U.S. and the U.K.

Harold L. Wolman

Lexington Books
D.C. Heath and Company
Lexington, Massachusetts
Toronto   London

British Crown copyright material was reproduced with the permission of the Controller of Her Britannic Majesty's Stationery Office

Library of Congress Cataloging in Publication Data

Wolman, Harold.
   Housing and housing policy in the U.S. and the U.K.

   Includes index.
   1. Housing–United States. 2. Housing–Great Britain. I. Title.
HD7293.W594   301.5'4'0942   74-25064
ISVN 0-669-97220-7

Copyright © 1975 by D.C. Heath and Company.

All rights reserved. No part of this publication may be reproduced or transmitted in any form or by any means, electronic or mechanical, including photocopy, recording, or any information storage or retrieval system, without permission in writing from the publisher.

Published simultaneously in Canada.

Printed in the United States of America.

International Standard Book Number: 0-669-97220-7

Library of Congress Catalog Card Number: 74-25064

To Dianne

Contents

	List of Tables	xi
	Acknowledgments	xiii
	Introduction	xv
Chapter 1	**The Context of Housing Policy**	3
	Ideological Assumptions Concerning the Rights and Responsibilities of Citizenship	3
	Economic Traditions	4
	Social Policy	4
	Differences in Political Structure	5
	Finance Systems	6
	Historical Development	7
	Political Cleavages Surrounding Housing Politics	7
	Perceptions of the Housing Problem	8
	Housing Standards and Quality	10
	Relative Wealth	10
	Housing and Politics	11
	Tenure	12
Chapter 2	**Housing as a Social Service**	15
Chapter 3	**Public Housing**	21
	Size and Scope	21
	Finance	26
	Public Housing as a Social Service—Tenant Selection and Characteristics	31
	The Siting of Public Housing	35
	Quasi-Public Sector Housing	36
	Summary and Conclusion	39

Chapter 4	**Private Rental Housing**	41
	Rent Control	41
	Size and Scope of the Private Rental Sector	47
	Condition of the Private Rental Sector	50
	Remedies	54
	Summary	60
Chapter 5	**Security of Tenure**	61
Chapter 6	**Rent Subsidies and Allowances**	67
Chapter 7	**Homeownership**	75
	House Purchase Prices	77
	Homeownership Costs	78
	Mortgage Costs and Institutions	79
	Consumer Protection	82
	Summary	83
Chapter 8	**Maintenance of the Housing Stock**	85
	Code Enforcement	85
	Improvements, Repairs, and Rehabilitation	90
Chapter 9	**The Role of Local Government**	95
	The Housing Role	95
	Housing and Planning	102
Chapter 10	**Conclusion**	105
	Public Sector Housing	105
	The Private Rental Sector	109
	Owner-Occupancy	111
	The Role of Local Government	112
	Conclusion	114

Notes	115
Index	123
About the Author	127

List of Tables

1-1	Tenure Status of Households in the United States and the United Kingdom, 1972	13
3-1	Public Sector Starts in Great Britain, 1963-1973	22
3-2	Public Sector Housing Activity in Great Britain, 1966-1973	25
3-3	U.S. Housing Starts, 1961-1973	25
3-4	Income Limits for U.S. Public Housing for a Family of Four, 1972	32
3-5	Public Housing Households in the United States and the United Kingdom, by Income Distribution, 1972	34
4-1	Stock of Dwellings in Great Britain, by Tenure, 1947-1972	47
4-2	U.S. Private Rental Units as a Percent of Total Units, 1900-1970	48
7-1	Owner-Occupancy in the United Kingdom, 1972	76
7-2	Cost of Homeownership in the United States, 1972	78
8-1	House Improvement Grants in Great Britain, 1966-1973	90

Acknowledgments

This book was researched and written during the last half of 1973 and first half of 1974 while the author was in London on a research fellowship provided by the National Endowment for the Humanities. In London the Centre for Environmental Studies (CES) was kind enough to allow me to use their facilities as a visiting scholar, and I would like to give special thanks to the Centre, its director David Donnison, and its staff for the advice and assistance they gave to me. Several people have read parts or all of the manuscript and made helpful suggestions and comments and I would like to publicly acknowledge my gratitude for their efforts. In addition to David Donnison, these include Jennifer Stoker, Richard Minns, Jane Morton, Alan Evans, Robin Thompson, and David Smith of the Centre; Della Nevitt and Peter Levin of the London School of Economics; David McKay of Essex University; Lou Rosenburg of the Planning Exchange, Lee Bromberg of Boston University, and Dianne Miller Wolman, my wife. Father Paul Byrne of the Shelter Housing Aid Centre both gave useful advice and graciously allowed me to spend two days interviewing his staff. Finally Frederiecke Taylor, Neil Pearcy, Molly Kershaw, and Mary Moody, all of the CES staff, Bunny Lopez, Secretary of the Politics II department of the University of Massachusetts—Boston and Carol Rosen, my assistant there, all provided diverse forms of assistance without which it would have been impossible to have pursued and completed this project. To all of the above and many more I give my heartfelt thanks.

Introduction

Cross-national comparisons of public policy serve several purposes. For the social scientist they provide the basis for building theories to explain public policy in different national settings and perhaps ultimately to develop some universal laws of public policy. But cross-national comparisons may also be quite useful to policy analysts or practitioners in the countries examined as well as to social scientists. There are several reasons why this might be true. First, the comparison may provide the practitioner with a contrast or a standard for evaluation in order that he may better understand or judge his own country's policies. Second, it may suggest a new framework or perspective for viewing problems or policy responses. Third, a comparative study may set forth alternatives that have not been considered, problems that have not yet been dealt with (or perceived as such), or gaps in coverage or policy that have not yet been recognized. Finally, such an approach may offer lessons from experience in an area where one country has utilized a policy approach that might be appropriate in the other.

In short, cross-national comparisons, by forcing a policy analyst or practitioner within a particular system to view that system against different standards than he usually does can throw new light on the strengths and weaknesses of existing policy, and, by suggesting a new way of looking at things, can provide the impetus for creative thinking and innovation. Housing is a policy area where far too little comparative work has been done, particularly so far as the United States—which tends to be quite insular with respect to its domestic policies—is concerned. This comparison of housing policy in the U.S. and the U.K. is directed towards filling this gap and towards providing policy analysts in both countries with the fruits of cross-national research described above.

Note: Throughout this book money values are expressed in the currency utilized by each country. Thus U.S. money values are expressed in terms of dollars and British money values in terms of pounds. During the year in which this book was written, the value of the dollar relative to the pound fluctuated from $2.60 to $2.15. However, in converting the value of one currency to the other, it is simplest—and does no grave damage to reality—to adopt the convention that one pound (£1) equals about $2.40 and one dollar ($1) equals about 42 pence (42 p).

Housing and Housing Policy in the U.S. and the U.K.

1 The Context of Housing Policy

Housing policy can only be understood, at least in comparative terms, if it is first placed firmly in the political, social, and economic context in which it exists in each country. This chapter is devoted to briefly setting forth the most salient features of this comparative context.

Ideological Assumptions Concerning the Rights and Responsibilities of Citizenship

In the United States the individual is thought to be primarily responsible for his own destiny. The role of the state is essentially to assure that equality of opportunity exists so that each citizen has an equal chance of achieving as much as his talents permit. Thus, government has traditionally played a strong role both in providing free public education (equality of opportunity) and in assuring that the rules of the game are adhered to. It has not traditionally played a major role in providing basic necessities as "rights of citizenship" to all citizens; rather it has selectively made these "basic necessities" available only to citizens who are not able to provide for themselves and usually in return for an acceptance of some responsibility of citizenship corresponding to this limited right. Americans are expected, if at all possible, to provide for their own housing. It is deemed right and just that individuals who have greater income should be able to use it to purchase correspondingly better housing than less successful (not fortunate; successful) citizens.

This ideological tradition is not totally foreign to the United Kingdom, but it is probably more descriptive of the social philosophy of Victorian England than that of the present time. The postwar "Welfare State" philosophy postulates that certain "basic necessities" are to be provided as rights of citizenship; the corresponding responsibilities of citizenship are much more vague than in the United States.[a] Also an emphasis on equality of results rather than mere equality of opportunity as the goal of government policy has become an increasingly important element of social philosophy among a growing segment of British

---
[a]In fact, a strong element of social theory in the United Kingdom suggests that there are no corresponding responsibilities, that the relationship between the state and the citizen is, in effect a gift relationship. See Richard Titmuss, *The Gift Relationship* (London: Penguin, 1970), chapter 5, pp. 12-14.

opinion since World War II. Thus, whereas in America concern tends to focus on the inadequate housing of poor people, in Britain concern is also centered on the inequitable distribution of the housing stock and housing services. Perhaps this is a subtle distinction, but psychologically and politically it does not seem so. The former concern suggests public policy should be directed towards enlarging the pie with particular attention given towards directing the increment towards the poor; the latter concern presents, in addition, the option of redistribution of the pie without enlargement.

Economic Traditions

Inextricably intertwined with these social ideologies are differing economic traditions. There is a tradition of public ownership in the United Kingdom that does not exist in the United States. The U.S. economy emphasizes private ownership; it is not, however, a free market or a laissez faire economy. Government intervention to promote public goals is common and accepted, but the intervention is more likely to occur within a framework of private ownership. In housing, for example, although a public sector exists, it is quite small. Nonetheless, federal government intervention has included the insuring of private mortgage loans on easy terms since 1934; the establishment of a secondary mortgage market to assure mortgage credit availability; the direct subsidization of mortgage repayments for some low- and moderate-income housing; the provision of strong tax incentives for investment in rental housing and even stronger ones for owner-occupancy; and the availability of rent supplements to a limited number of tenants in privately owned housing.

Social Policy

Given the above, it is not surprising that social policy in the United States is largely designed to play a derivative and residual role. Americans are expected to provide for their needs themselves. If they are unable to do so, then the government, in an increasing number of areas, assures that their needs are met. Thus, social policy is "selective"—that is, it applies only to the residual not able to provide for themselves and utilizes a means test to identify who those are. In addition, when assistance is made available, the standard normally provided is minimally adequate or sufficient rather than one equal to that of those not receiving assistance. There is strong social consensus that while no American should lack the basic necessities, those who provide for themselves deserve to be better off than those who receive government assistance.

The social philosophy of the British welfare state differs sharply from the American conception of welfare. Reacting against centuries of Poor Law administration with its institutionalized stigma and hated means test, there is now substantial—though not complete—agreement that the most basic social needs should be provided by the state as a right, on a universalistic basis, and with no means test. Furthermore, the standard provided should be equal to, or in excess of, that provided in the private sector. Obviously, budgetary constraints make this impossible in many cases, including housing. Thus some sort of mechanism is needed to allocate limited resources. In the area of income support, means tests are still utilized. In housing, the concept of housing need, which is not necessarily synonymous with low income, is utilized.

In actual practice, American social policy is not *as* harsh nor British policy *as* beneficent as the contrasting philosophies underpinning those policies would suggest. In fact, the similarity in social policies is often striking despite the ideological differences. Nonetheless, it would be a mistake to assume that these differences on the philosophical level are unimportant or that public policy in action is ultimately disconnected from them. Rather, they help to throw light upon many of the differences in social policy, including housing policy, between the two countries. In particular, they help to account for the emphasis on housing as a social service in British housing policy and the relative lack of such emphasis in the United States. This difference—one of the most important and fundamental between the two countries—is considered of sufficient importance to be treated in a separate chapter (see Chapter 2).

Differences in Political Structure

The United Kingdom is a unitary system with a national government exercising sovereignty and with local authorities existing as the creatures of national government. Thus, constitutionally, national government can mandate local government action or it can provide local government with the discretionary authority to take action. Local governments are proscribed from taking any action not expressly permitted by the central government. However, in actual practice wide authority for the operation of some functions, including, at least traditionally, housing, has been assigned to local authorities. Because this devolution of authority has come to be accepted as proper, it is politically much less easy for the central government to mandate local authorities to undertake activities against their will than it might seem from a mechanical understanding of the constitutional arrangements.

Nonetheless central control is surely easier to achieve in the United Kingdom than in the United States. The American system is federal with the federal government and the states sharing sovereignty. While local governments exist as the creatures of state governments, most states nonetheless allow their localities broad—though not complete—discretion to devise their own policies. The federal government, generally speaking, may encourage state or local action by making federal funds available or by making receipt of federal funds for some other purpose contingent upon certain action being taken, but the government cannot mandate or prevent such action unless it is constitutionally required or proscribed or unless it involves activities crossing state boundaries.[b] For these reasons, it is much easier to implement a consistent social policy nationwide in the United Kingdom than it is in the United States.

Given these differences in political structure, it is quite surprising that housing policy is seen as a local responsibility in the United Kingdom, while it is largely a federal responsibility, with little local participation or interest, in the United States. However, in the United Kingdom housing policy is a local responsibility because it is assigned as one by the national government and accepted as one by local authorities, and given the housing needs of their constituency, most local authorities find acceptance of this responsibility politically beneficial. In the United States, housing policy has been a federal responsibility because local governments have not taken responsibility for it. They have not done so largely because the politics of housing promise liabilities rather than benefits at the polls for elected officials who attempt to confront housing problems.

Thus, in the United States, the federal government has responded to a need not being met at the state or local level. Local governments devise and administer housing codes and zoning ordinances and—through a semi-autonomous local housing authority usually appointed by a mayor but not removable by him—run the quite small (relative to the United Kingdom's) public housing program. But overall concern for housing—and most programs and initiatives—has emanated from Washington. In fact, much of recent American housing policy has tended to bypass state and local governments completely by providing subsidies from the federal government directly to private builders, investors, owners, or tenants. It is indeed ironic that in the United States, with its tradition of decentralization and local control, a seemingly local function such as housing should be so ignored at the local level and so focused at the federal level, while in the United Kingdom, where centralization of authority is the fundamental constitutional arrangement, the contrary has been true.

Finance Systems

British local authorities receive a much greater portion of their general revenues from the central government than do American cities from state and federal governments. In 1971, local authorities received 58 percent of their tax revenues in the form of intergovernment grants compared to 30 percent for their American counterparts. American cities are thus forced to depend upon their

[b]In this case, federal action is permissible under the Interstate Commerce clause of the U.S. Constitution.

own tax bases that have been continually shrinking as middle- and high-income whites migrate to the suburbs. The demands upon the consequently inadequate, locally derived tax revenue are also steadily increasing because of the severity of problems caused by the concentration of poor and minority households within city boundaries. So it is not a simple task for American cities to generate internally new funds for housing programs.

Historical Development

Any discussion of the context in which housing policy exists cannot ignore the differences in the historical underpinnings of that policy in the two countries. British housing policy derives initially from the public health movement of the nineteenth century, which lead to legislation permitting local authorities to provide sanitary housing for working-class citizens. The first legislation, in fact, specified that Poor Law recipients were ineligible for this housing.[c] The major expansion of local authority housing, including the first legislation providing central government subsidies, occurred in response to the acute housing shortage resulting from the First World War, when an immense campaign was undertaken to provide homes for heroes—the returning soldiers. The same process was repeated after World War II. In both cases, an immense effort was needed simply to provide enough houses for people to live in. American housing policy, on the other hand, derives from the depression of the 1930s and its prime motive was to invigorate the deflated construction industry and to protect the mortgage market, rather than to remedy an acute housing shortage. The public sector housing that was to be built as a result of the former motive was to be occupied by the poorest and most unfortunate members of the society.

British policy thus flowed from a national effort to adequately house a broad sector of the community, particularly after periods of crisis. The occupants of public sector housing were seen as ordinary working people, self-sufficient and capable, but unable to be housed during an acute housing shortage. In the United States, policy derived not from a national effort to rehouse people made homeless by an external event clearly not of their making, but from macro level efforts to revive a depressed economy and to protect investor confidence. Occupants were not seen to be the ordinary man, but the unfortunate few.

Political Cleavages Surrounding Housing Politics

The foregoing should not imply that public sector housing is not a political issue in the United Kingdom, for it clearly is and has been. But the cleavage

---
[c]I am indebted to Jane Morton of the Centre for Environmental Studies for this information.

surrounding the issue is on a much different dimension than it is in the United States. In the United Kingdom, the cleavage is class, while in the United States it is race. Public sector housing in the United Kingdom is viewed predominantly as working-class housing (although the range of occupants does span the socioeconomic spectrum), and the politics of council housing are quite often explicable along class lines. These political differences are not normally concerned with the *existence* of a substantial public sector, but with questions of subsidization formulas, rent levels, siting, and so forth.

In the United States, public housing politics have become largely racial politics, to the great detriment of the viability of the program. Public housing is viewed by most Americans, with increasing accuracy, as housing for the non-white population. As such, all the fears, prejudices, hopes and ideals that the American people bring to the problem of race relations and racial integration are focused on public housing. This applies also, although markedly less strongly, to American attitudes towards federally subsidized programs other than public housing. It may well be that there is a strong element of class division residing behind and motivating the racial division; the question is difficult to disentangle given the economic status of black Americans. Nonetheless, the fact that it is discussed and perceived in racial terms creates a much different form of politics and much different results.

Public housing in the United States arouses strong emotions—much stronger than those aroused in the United Kingdom. Lack of support for public sector housing in the United Kingdom because of class divisions and opposition to class integration does exist and is real. However, on the whole, this opposition is not based on the threat and fear of the unknown and alien that characterize white attitudes in the United States toward racial integration with its consequent (in their minds) rapid neighborhood deterioration, crime, and vandalism. In many American cities, the opposition to public housing based on these fears has resulted in the concentration into huge high-rise public housing blocks of large numbers of problem families and dependent families, particularly female-headed black families on welfare. The consequence has been to intensify and make worse the very situation that was feared in the first place. As a result, dislike of public housing—or rather its residents—is shared not only by most whites but by stable, middle-class and working-class blacks as well. It is important to note—and this point is argued further in Chapter 3—that this fear of and opposition to public housing is based much more on the characteristics of its residents rather than on ideological obduracy with respect to the involvement of the public sector.

Perceptions of the Housing Problem

The way British policy makers perceive their housing problem is colored by the housing shortage the country has chronically faced and by the large numbers of old houses constantly falling below changing societal standards of adequacy. The housing problem in the United Kingdom is pre-eminently seen therefore as a problem of the housing stock—its size and physical condition. Recently income and class distribution of the housing stock as well as housing opportunities have also become a concern, particularly among Labour Party-oriented policy makers. Popular concern tends to focus on emotive issues such as homelessness (a derivative of housing shortage) and inadequate security of tenure and high rents, particularly in London and other large urban areas.

In the United States, housing problems are seen by many policy makers in quite different perspectives. Housing is seen as one link in a cycle of deprivation that enmeshes poor people and particularly blacks and minorities. As such, it is viewed as related to the entire neighborhood environment—slums rather than unfit houses—and to the public services provided in that environment. Many American observers may well agree with former HUD Secretary Romney's comments that successful housing policy is impossible except in a context of a policy that creates a viable neighborhood environment, including adequate public services. Thus Anthony Downs reflects the developing conventional wisdom when he writes:

The most serious urban housing problems involve many factors other than physical dwelling units, including income poverty that prevents millions of households from being able to pay for decent housing; high-quality local housing standards that exclude the poor from living in more prosperous areas; destructive personal behavior patterns exhibited by a small percentage of the residents in concentrated poverty areas that make their neighborhoods undesirable places in which to live; and middle-class withdrawal that takes place in and near concentrated poverty areas. Experience proves that attempts to combat the most serious urban housing problems are certain to fail unless they respond effectively to these factors, as well as to needs for physical dwelling units.[1]

This approach appears to be in accord with the actual concerns of residents of poor housing. On the basis of two attitude surveys of Baltimore residents, Louis Rosenburg reports:

The most striking finding concerning attitudes towards the residential environment is that consistently throughout the first and second household surveys, the number of respondents who expressed serious dissatisfaction with regard to quality of neighborhood exceeded the number who expressed similar feelings about the quality of their dwelling unit. In the initial household survey, this differential was suggested by respondents' perception of neighborhood safety as compared with their attitudes towards the home. Whereas only one respondent in ten expressed dislike for his (her) present dwelling unit, one in four considered the neighborhood unsafe. Within the inner city, the corresponding relationship was slightly more pronounced; 13 percent of the residents were dissatisfied with their homes, as against 35 percent who viewed their immediate areas as unsafe. . . .
    The results of the second survey point up not only the comparatively greater disenchantment with the environment than with the dwelling, but also how

widespread are negative attitudes towards quality of neighborhood among residents in poorer sections of the city....

Turning to the specific sources of discontent and concern, the results of the second household survey show that, in the inner city, three aspects of the residential environment—lack of play areas for small children..., noise, and robberies and other crimes—were regarded as major problems by three respondents in ten. Six additional aspects of neighborhood quality—condition of other housing on block, street cleaning, neighborhood shopping, traffic, police protection and abandoned housing/littered lots—were perceived as seriously inadequate by from one-sixth to one-fifth of the low-income households located in the inner city. Surprisingly, schools were considered a big problem by fewer than one person in ten.[2]

Housing Standards and Quality

Although cross-national comparisons are quite difficult, it seems safe to conclude that the average housing unit in the United States is of higher standard and costs less in relation to average income than does its U.K. counterpart. At the same time, it is equally relevant to point out that the worst housing in the United States is probably of lower quality than its U.K. counterpart and that the festering slums and deteriorating neighborhoods in many American inner-city areas represent a condition more intense and distressing than slum neighborhoods in the United Kingdom.

In terms of space, the average American home is substantially larger than the average English one. Data on this is sketchy, but the average "improved" floor area in new, FHA-insured, one-family houses in 1971 (this serves primarily the lower-middle income sector) was 117.8 square meters; the average floor space in new private dwellings insured in the United Kingdom by the Nationwide Building Society in 1970 was 82.54 square meters and the average for new local authority dwellings built in 1971 was only 68.1 square meters.[3]

By all accounts, American homes are better heated and insulated as well. As far as other amenities are concerned, the 1970 U.S. census disclosed that 5.5 percent of all occupied housing units in the United States lacked some or all plumbing facilities, whereas the 1971 House Condition Survey showed that 15.8 percent of all U.K. occupied units lacked one or more of these basic amenities. However, according to the socially defined standards of standard housing peculiar to each society, the percentage of substandard housing in the U.S. (7.6 percent) nearly matches the percentage of unfit housing in the U.K. (7.3 percent).[4] Finally, the median age of the English housing stock (about 45 years) is considerably older than that in the United States (about 35 years).

Relative Wealth

The United States is a much wealthier country than the United Kingdom. Not only can it afford to invest more in housing, it apparently is more willing to do so. Thus, although U.S. GNP per capita is roughly twice that of the United Kingdom, new housing investment per capita in the United States is about 3.3 times higher per capita than in the United Kingdom. Or, put another way, the United States spends a somewhat higher portion of its GNP on housing investment. The results are obvious: new units (excluding mobile homes) usually average between 2.25 and 3.0 percent of total housing stock in the United States (2.86 percent in 1972) compared to between 1.5 and 2.5 percent in Great Britain (1.7 percent in 1972). The average annual rate of new building completed in Great Britain was 2 percent of existing stock between 1967 and 1972, which represents a steady fall from a high of 2.30 percent in 1968 to a low of 1.70 percent in 1972. The average annual rate in the United States was 2.5 percent over a three-year period between 1970 and 1972. The average annual net addition to stock in the United Kingdom from 1966 to 1972 was about 1.5 percent compared to about 2.15 percent in the United States between 1970 and 1972. In both countries house building suffers severely from tight money policy designed to combat inflation as evidenced by the slump in housing starts in 1973 and 1974.

This data on housing investment is not totally divorced from longstanding attitudes concerning the portion of income that it is appropriate to spend for housing. In the United States, the budgetary rule of thumb is that a household should spend no more than 25 percent of its income for accommodation. In fact, in 1971, the median rent-income ratio in the privately rented sector in the United States was 20.9 percent. In the United Kingdom, there exists the expectation that rent should constitute a somewhat lower portion of income, which, in fact, it does. In 1972, the rent-income ratio for rental property, both private and public, was in the range of 11 percent, although this ratio—traditionally in the range of 7 to 8 percent—is now increasing rapidly.

Housing and Politics

Housing is a major political issue, both on the national and local levels, in the United Kingdom in a way that it is not in the United States. In the February 1974 general election, public opinion polls consistently showed 20 to 30 percent of the people considered housing an important issue in the campaign, exceeded in importance only by inflation. In the 1972 presidential election in the United States, housing was rarely mentioned as a major issue, and, according to polls, less than 10 percent considered it so.

On the local level, housing usually ranks as one of the two or three most important issues in the United Kingdom, whereas it is rarely a local issue at all in the United States, except in terms of segregation or integration. Housing is not viewed as an important municipal function, either by the city fathers or, apparently, by citizens. However much the latter may look upon their own housing conditions as unsatisfactory, they apparently do not perceive it as a problem for which local elected officials should be held responsible.

To some extent the relative size of the public sector in the two countries may help to account for the salience of housing as a political issue. When a substantial portion of the local council electorate (30 percent nationally, but an absolute majority in many local authorities) are council house tenants, that constitutes an important electoral block politicians dare not ignore in local elections. While council house tenants in the United Kingdom are thus a not unimportant force in shaping policy (or at least a visible constraint defining what actions cannot be taken), public housing tenants in the United States are acted upon by public policy and are thus mostly passive recipients.

The direct impact of tenants on public policy through elections is enhanced in the United Kingdom by the political structure of local housing authorities. These authorities are subcommittees of the locally elected authorities, and members are thus directly responsible to the electorate. In the United States, public housing authorities are independent appointive bodies whose members are not politically responsible (although if they were, the results might be quite detrimental to the interest of public housing tenants).

Tenure

In the United States, the vast majority of households are either owner-occupiers or renters of private dwelling units, while in the United Kingdom, the vast majority are either owner-occupiers or renters of public sector units, as can be seen in Table 1-1. These differences in the tenure status of households in each country are critical to an understanding of housing policies in the two countries and thus necessary to establish prior to beginning our analysis. The study has been divided loosely into sections corresponding to these various tenure arrangements.

Table 1-1
Tenure Status of Households in the United States and the United Kingdom, 1972

	Percent of Households	
	United States	United Kingdom
Owner-Occupier	62[a]	51
Private Rental	36[b]	18[c]
Public Rental	1.5%	31

[a]This figure includes 3 percent of all U.S. households who are resident in mobile homes or roughly what are called caravans in the United Kingdom. These mobile homes, because of their low cost, represent an increasingly important element of the housing stock in the United States, particularly for low- and lower-middle-income families. During the five-year period from 1969-1973, they represented more than 25 percent of all new housing.

[b]This includes about 1 percent that are privately owned but have been directly and heavily subsidized by the U.S. federal government.

[c]This includes about 5 percent that are owned by non-profit housing associations or housing societies and are sometimes considered public sector housing.

Source: Data derived from U.S., Department of Housing and Urban Development, *Housing in the Seventies* (Washington, D.C.: HUD, 1973), p. 6-3; and U.K., Central Statistical Office, *Social Trends*, HMSO, No. 4, 1973, p. 156.

2 Housing as a Social Service

One of the less visible, but nonetheless important differences between British and American housing policy—and one which itself greatly helps to account for many of the other differences—is the view each country holds with respect to the appropriate responsibility of government in meeting the shelter needs of its citizens. The concept of housing as a social service appears frequently in discussions of British housing policy, while it is not a common frame of reference for debate on American housing policy. While observers disagree on whether British housing policy meets the criterion of a social service, the most common view is that it possesses some elements unique to the social services but lacks others. T.H. Marshall concludes, for example:

The question was raised ... whether housing policy should be regarded as a social service. Part of the troubles experienced by British housing policy arise from the fact that it has found no clear answer to this question.[1]

The term appears frequently in partisan debates with the Left, in particular, arguing that the social service element is inadequate in existing policy and that this lack is a primary cause of the failure of that policy. Vigorous critiques of housing policy often conclude with an invocation to move towards a policy that treats housing as a real social service. There appears to be wide agreement, at least verbally, that public policy towards housing ought to be social service oriented; the debate centers more on whether, in fact, it is.

Unfortunately, there appears to be confusion over what the term housing as a social service really means. In some cases, it seems to be used merely as a synonym for the amount of housing in the public sector. At other times, it takes the form of a description of the management of the public sector stock. Is the public stock to be managed primarily by the criterion of economic efficiency or is it to be managed primarily to meet the social needs of those most in need within some budgetary constraint? Finally, it is sometimes used to refer to those activities undertaken by the society directed towards assuring that all citizens are adequately housed at a price they can afford, regardless of whether they are housed in the private or public sector.

For our purposes it is necessary to distinguish two related concepts. In the context of housing, a social service *philosophy* is adhered to to the extent that the state both recognizes and acknowledges a responsibility to assure that all its citizens are decently housed. A social service *approach* is pursued to the extent that the state undertakes activities directed towards implementing a social service philosophy. By decently housed, we mean not only that households be provided with a physically sound structure for shelter at a price within their means, but also of a suitable size and location given their needs, within a functioning and viable neighborhood environment, and with an adequate supply of housing-related services.

While in neither country is housing viewed completely as a social service given the above definitions, it appears clear that the social service philosophy is more widely held in the United Kingdom than in the United States, and the social service approach is much more prevalent in the United Kingdom. Government in Britain explicitly accepts some responsibility, through its local authorities, for the housing conditions of its citizens. In doing so, it reflects a much different conception of society's responsibilities to its members than that prevailing in the United States.

The scope of these responsibilities, at least in theory, is quite wide. A selection of statements from a government White Paper, "Widening the Choice: The Next Steps in Housing" (issued by the Conservative Government in 1971), is illustrative:

The ultimate aim of housing policy is that everyone should have a decent home with a reasonable choice of owning or renting the sort of home they want....
The social health of an area on the quality of its built environment, are largely determined by its housing. The Government therefore believes that local authorities should take a broad view of their statutory housing functions....
In response to the Government's request local authorities are drawing up 10-year strategies to discharge comprehensively their responsibility for dealing with unfit and sub-standard housing....
A wide view of local authority housing responsibilities is particularly necessary in considering those areas of stress where overcrowding and bad housing are worst. These are the areas where the housing stock is old and in poor condition and when the combination of acute physical and social problems makes action most difficult. In many of these areas—for example certain parts of London and other great cities—the decline of the private rented sector, and its relatively poor response to the incentives of improvement grants, threaten to perpetuate poor housing conditions and to increase social deprivation. Only a comprehensive approach will succeed in curing the ills of these areas.[2]

Spokesmen for the Labour Party are much more explicit about their view of government's responsibility for housing its citizens. Anthony Crosland, Labour's housing spokesman, writes:

But why should it be the responsibility of government to ensure that these various [housing] needs are met? Why do we not leave the provision of housing, as we do the provision of motor cars, to market forces and the play of supply and demand....
It must be possible—indeed it is in our view a basic right of citizenship—for every household, especially families with young children but also the growing

numbers of young married couples and pensioners, to have a minimum civilized standard of dwelling adequate for a decent, comfortable and private household life....

So we cannot have a market solution to the housing problem. Some part of the building program must be public; some part of the housing stock must be leased or owned at less than the economic cost; and the government must bear a final responsibility for the overall housing situation.[3]

As the above statements indicate, the Labour Party puts a great emphasis on fulfilling the government's social responsibility (which it also enunciates more clearly) through provision of public sector housing, while the Conservative Party views public sector housing more as one tool among many and perhaps one that has been overutilized. While the differences between the parties within the British context are significant, it is important to recognize that relative to the dominant ideology defining housing policy in the United States, both British parties—and British society as a whole—embrace, at least verbally, a social service philosophy of housing: the government is responsible for the housing conditions of its citizens.

But how and to what extent is this social service philosophy translated into a social service approach? The most current expression of the attempt to implement this social service ideology through a social service approach is found in the effort to create a "comprehensive housing service" by reorienting the present local housing authorities. Thus, David Donnison writes that the aims of a comprehensive housing service should be

... to extend opportunities—to try so far as possible, to help people get the housing they want, where they want it, whether it be to rent or to buy, whether they have large families or live by themselves, whether the house be an improved old one or a good new one. We also aim to assure a minimum standard of privacy, security and comfort for all at a price they can pay.[4]

Proponents of the comprehensive housing approach wish to expand the long-standing and traditional statement of the British social service approach that imposes a statutory duty upon local governments

... to consider housing conditions in their district and the needs of their district with respect to the provision of further housing accommodation ... and to prepare and submit to the Minister proposals for the provision of new houses.[5]

Most local authorities have interpreted this statement of a social service approach almost completely in terms of the construction, management, and allocation of public housing, to which they have traditionally devoted the bulk of their efforts.

As the above discussion implies, not only is housing regarded *more* as a social service in the United Kingdom than in the United States, but again in contrast to the United States, it is regarded primarily as a locally provided and administered social service. Thus, John Macey, past president of the Institute of Housing Managers, observes:

The town or city council is the primary authority for housing which is run in the United Kingdom just like any other service such as the fire service.[6]

The central government has placed responsibility for meeting housing needs primarily on local authorities. They pursue these responsibilities within a framework of subsidies, regulations, and legally defined property rights set by the central government.

In the United States there is less of a tradition of viewing housing as a social right that government must provide for its citizens. This is true despite the apparently explicit adoption of a social service philosophy in the Housing Act of 1949 (reaffirmed again in 1968), which posited "a decent home in a suitable living environment for all Americans" as a national goal. Unfortunately, it is not clear what interpretation to put upon this statement. Was it meant to be a commitment for government action or merely a pious expression of desire? In any case, no systematic social service approach was set up to implement that goal.

According to the first interpretation, the government has, by the 1949 Declaration, embraced the concept of government responsibility for the housing conditions of its citizens—that is, a social service philosophy—but has, in fact, pursued this goal sporadically and as only one of several somewhat divergent and competing goals for its housing policy. (Others include support of the home-building sector of the economy, development of an effective and stable set of mortgage market institutions, economic stabilization—in which housing policy is usually perceived as a counter cyclical tool to that end—slum clearance and urban redevelopment, and welfare assistance for those unable to find housing in the private market.[a]

Furthermore the housing social service goal has been given low priority relative to other competing uses for public sector resources. From 1965 to 1972, total federal government spending for all housing and community development activities (including urban renewal and poverty programs as well as housing) was only 1.5 percent of total federal budgetary outlays. If defense expenditures are eliminated, housing and community development activities still amounted to only 2.6 percent of remaining outlays. State and local governments added a very

---

[a]Anthony Downs lists 10 major objectives pursued by federal housing policy: (1) high level overall housing production; (2) adequate housing finance; (3) reduced housing costs; (4) overall economic stabilization; (5) stabilization of housing production; (6) attraction of private capital; (7) housing assistance to low- and moderate-income households; (8) increased home ownership; (9) improved inner-city conditions; and (10) creation of good new neighborhoods. See Downs, "The Successes and Failures of Federal Housing Policy," *The Public Interest*, Winter 1974, p. 125.

small amount from their own funds to the federal figures. In 1970, housing and urban renewal together accounted for less than 1 percent of all public sector expenditure.[7] (In the same year housing accounted for 5.8 percent of all public sector expenditure in the United Kingdom.)[8]

Further evidence for the low priority given housing in the United States lies in the relatively small proportion of the housing stock that is federally owned or subsidized (about 3.3 percent) and the paucity and ineffectiveness of other activities that have been undertaken to achieve the social service goal. In short, according to this interpretation, the U.S. government has accepted the social service philosophy (although it surely is not nearly as *widely* accepted either by public officials or by citizens in the United States as in the United Kingdom) but has not adopted a social service approach for it has not undertaken many activities necessary to implement the social service philosophy. To a large extent this is due to the real lack of consensus on the social service goal itself and to its acceptance as only one—and not necessarily the primary one—among competing housing goals.

The second interpretation sees the 1949 Declaration merely as an expression of a desirable state of affairs, but one that government does not bear the final responsibility for bringing about. This should not be misinterpreted to imply that the government has been all but inactive in the area of housing or has simply left it to free market forces, for that has clearly not been the case. In fact, since 1949—really since 1937—a variety of policies and programs have addressed themselves to housing problems, and many of these efforts contain elements of a social service approach. But the general context in which housing policy is made does not assume a government responsibility to ensure all Americans have minimally adequate housing. Enlightened social policy may be directed to bringing about that condition, but it is not a responsibility in the sense that minimum standards of education, fire protection and, increasingly, income are perceived as government responsibilities—albeit mostly local or state government responsibilities.

Perhaps both interpretations are correct at different times. But the result is the same in either case. Housing policy in the United States is not characterised by a social service approach to the same extent it is in the United Kingdom. Part of the reason for this clearly is the lack of consensus on (according to interpretation 1) or acceptance of (according to interpretation 2) the social service philosophy in the United States. As pointed out in Chapter 1, ideological differences concerning the appropriate role of government in the economy, the degree to which the government or the individual is responsible for providing for the individual's well-being, and the willingness to accept private market determined distributions of income and housing opportunities as just and equitable divide the two countries. However, the difference may also be partly due to government structure, and particularly, the division of functions between various levels of government.

So far we have contended that the concept of housing as a social service is more engrained in the United Kingdom than in the United States, although housing policy in the United States is certainly not devoid of social service elements. We have also seen that insofar as the social service concept exists, it is perceived far more as a municipal function in the United Kingdom than in the United States. Now let us turn to the devices and instruments each society uses to pursue social service objectives.

As has already been noted, many of these devices are implemented by the local authority in the United Kingdom. They include: (1) the building and administration of public (council) housing; (2) a system of means-tested rent subsidies (rent rebates for public housing tenants and rent allowances for the private rental sector); (3) rent control and regulation in the private rental sector coupled with legislation providing security of tenure, at least for residents of the private unfurnished rental sector; (4) power to enforce minimum basic standards in private housing through compulsory purchase and repair orders; (5) control of unfit housing through repair or demolition orders; (6) the availability of improvement grants to rehabilitate or improve privately and publicly owned housing; (7) direct mortgage loans for low-income purchasers and subsidized mortgages for low-income people (option mortgages); (8) a system of temporary accommodation for the homeless; (9) welfare payments (supplementary benefits) for housing purposes to the poor; and (10) Housing Advice Centres designed to provide free advice and, at times, assistance to anyone in the local authority with a housing problem.

In the United States, social service devices include: (1) the building and administration of public housing by the local housing authority; (2) code enforcement by the city; (3) quite limited programs of direct mortgage interest rate subsidies for low-income home purchasers and rental assistance run by the federal government; (4) similarly limited rehabilitation grants and loans provided by the federal government; (5) public assistance payments for the poor, which already provide, in many states, a form of housing allowance; (6) and federal support of various mortgage market institutions designed to assure a ready supply of mortgage funds on reasonable terms.

While most of these devices can be considered primarily social service in nature, in neither country do they amount to a fully coordinated social service approach, although they come much nearer to being so in the United Kingdom than they do in the United States, nor have they all been unambiguously successful. In some cases, it may well be that some of these "social service approaches" have had unintended second-order effects that have resulted in diminishing rather than improving housing well-being. Within the framework of our analysis of tenure sectors, we shall pay particularly attention to these various social service approaches and their successes and failures.

3 Public Housing

Public housing (or council housing as it is termed in the United Kingdom) has a long and honorable tradition in the United Kingdom in a way that it does not in the United States. This is due not only to cultural and ideological differences with respect to the proper role of the public sector and the responsibility of the state to its citizens but also to the circumstances of the programs' origins in both countries.

In the United Kingdom, the impetus for public housing on a widespread scale was the dire housing shortage caused by the havoc wrought by two world wars and the consequent need to rehouse rapidly the large numbers of citizens and returning soldiers, who literally had no place to live in the aftermath. The genesis of public housing in the United States, on the other hand, was primarily in the need to rescue the construction and home-building industry in the depths of the 1930s depression and secondarily to help the most unfortunate citizens who could not afford housing available on the free market. Thus, the British program was conceived of as a concerted national effort to rehouse the British people, while the American program was conceived of as a spur to the construction industry and as a social responsibility to the poor. In both countries housing policy continues to reflect these initial orientations.

Size and Scope

As of 1973, 30.7 percent of all housing units in the United Kingdom were public housing (53 percent in Scotland),[1] and over the six-year period from 1968-1973 37.3 percent of all new starts have been in the public sector.[2] A sizeable public sector is accepted by both political parties, although the Labour Party favors expanding the public sector, while the Conservatives generally wish to maintain it as its present portion of the housing stock or to reduce it slightly. Thus, the Conservatives advocate the sale of existing council housing to sitting tenants at easy terms (a similar program called "Turnkey" exists in the U.S.), while the Labour Party decries this device as a means of permanently reducing the stock of housing that the public sector can allocate according to social need rather than market criteria.[a] Nonetheless, as Table 3-1 indicates, public sector starts as a portion of total starts are substantial both under Labour and Conservative governments.

The data clearly indicates that public housing starts have represented a substantial portion of housing activity under governments of both parties. Indeed, partisan rhetoric during election time notwithstanding, it is difficult to draw any clear conclusion from the aggregate national data presented below concerning the type of government under which public sector activity fares better, even though it has been charged that the fall in council house starts since 1970 can be ascribed to an unsympathetic Tory Government.

First, the decision to build a council dwelling unit is initiated locally, not by the central government (as is also true of public housing in the United States). Local authorities, of course, vary in the political complexion of their councils, but it is not unusual for the majority of local councils to be controlled by the

Table 3-1
Public Sector Starts in Great Britain, 1963-1973

		Number of Public Housing Starts (in Thousands)	Public Housing Starts as Percent of Total Starts
Conservative (1963-64)	1963	168.6	45.8
	1964	178.6	41.9
	1965	181.4	46.2
Labour (1965-70)	1966	185.9	49.0
	1967	213.9	47.8
	1968	194.3	49.2
	1969	176.6	51.4
Transition	1970	154.1	48.3
	1971	136.6	39.7
Conservative (1970-73)	1972	123.0	35.1
	1973	112.8	34.4[a]

[a]The public sector starts are slightly inflated because housing association starts are included. See Chapter 3 for a description of housing associations. The above figures include starts by New Town corporations and government departments as well as local authorities.
Source: U.K., Department of Environment, *Housing and Construction Statistics*, HMSO, No. 8, 4th Quarter, 1973, p. 19.

---

[a]Nearly 45,000 such sales took place by local authorities during 1972 under strong encouragement from the Conservative Central Government. These sales averaged about 7,500 per year during the last 3 years of the Labour Government (1968-1970). See U.K., Department of Environment, *Housing and Construction Statistics*, HMSO, No. 7, 3rd Quarter, 1973, p. 48.

party in opposition in Parliament.[b] Central governments do have the means to encourage or discourage local decisions concerning their house-building activity, but civil servants interviewed at the Department of Environment insist, although they are disputed by some outside observers, that governments of both parties have consistently urged local authorities to build more during the past decade. The most direct mechanism for central government control lies in the requirement that local housing authorities must apply for and receive central government permission in order to borrow funds in the capital market. This means that the central government potentially has the ability both to control the total number of starts in the public sector and to allocate this total among the local authorities. However, in recent years, it appears that approval has been granted in a pro forma fashion. Another source of central government control is the cost yardstick. Since 1967, local authorities have not been able to build housing exceeding a central government-set cost yardstick that has lagged seriously behind inflation. However, local authorities wishing to build housing in excess of the yardstick cost may apply to the government for permission to do so. Apparently this permission has been liberally granted. Nonetheless, high costs have made local authorities chary of building during the past few years, and the cost yardstick plus fixed-price rather than cost-plus contracts have made it difficult for many local authorities to find builders willing to work for them.

Secondly, as the cost of construction increases, local authorities—many of which have come under stinging attack recently for slum clearance and building programs that have destroyed existing neighborhoods—are increasingly switching their resources into housing rehabilitation through use of improvement grants (see Chapter 8), which activity is not reflected in Table 3-1. They have generally been encouraged by governments of both parties in this undertaking. Thus, in 1968, a White Paper issued by the Labour Government announced that "the balance of need between new house building and improvement is now changing so there must be a corresponding change in the emphasis of the local authority housing programmes. The Government intend that within a total of public investment in housing at about the level it has now reached, a greater share should go to the improvement of older houses."[3] As Trevor Roberts points out:

it was not clearly recognized at the time that the Government, a Labour Government, was unambiguously proposing to cut down the level of housebuilding and, what is more, to do this by cutting the level of council housing. A leading Labour expert on housing has ascribed the curtailment of council house building to the widespread takeover of local councils by the Conservatives in May, 1968 (Allaun, *No Place Like Home*, London, 1972, p. 194). He fails to recognize that the Conservative councils were implementing, albeit without any reluctance, the Labour Government's national policy. Interestingly enough, the decline in council house building has continued despite the more recent recovery of many councils by the Labour Party.[4]

---

[b]Local council elections do not coincide with Parliamentary elections but are held instead at regular three-year intervals.

The impact of the decision to change priorities is dramatically demonstrated by Table 3-2.

Finally, governments of both parties have tended to discourage or restrict council house starts as a counter-inflationary measure during times of economic crises.

In the United States, public housing as of December 31, 1972, accounted for only 1.5 percent of the 68,500,000 housing units in the country, although in large cities it may be substantially more. In addition, the United States developed a system during the 1960s of heavily federally subsidized, but privately owned, housing that accounts for another 1.8 percent of the housing stock. Neither of these figures includes housing financed through federally guaranteed or insured private mortgages that comprise probably 15 to 20 percent of the present housing stock; however, it would be difficult to include these within the framework of a social service approach.[c] Since the Housing Act of 1968, which was designed to encourage—through publicly provided subsidies—substantial private investment in lower-income housing and which was passed with bipartisan support, public sector activity (both publicly owned and subsidized) has greatly increased. Between 1969 and 1972, the public sector accounted for 23 percent of new units started, with a height of 29 percent reached in 1970.[d] Thus, during the past five years, the tradition of a largely inactive U.S. public sector housing effort has been shattered. As Table 3-3 indicates, federally subsidized activity during 1970 and 1971 actually exceeded, in absolute terms, total housing starts, both public and private, in the United Kingdom during the same period.

---

[c]This program, administered through the Federal Housing Administration (FHA), which is now a constituent part of the Department of Housing and Urban Development (HUD), provides federal insurance to back up mortgage loans for qualifying home buyers. Its initial raison d'etre lies in the depression when mortgage money was nearly unavailable because of the high risk of default and foreclosure during a time of falling property values. By insuring the lender against loss, the mortgage insurance relieves him of risk and encourages the ready availability of mortgage money. In return, the government requires that the mortgage terms be quite easy—low down payment and long-term amortization. For most of FHA's history, its clients have been lower-middle-income and middle-income families rather than poor families. The latter have not qualified because the mortgage insurance, until quite recently, was only to be granted to mortgagees who were sound economic risks; in any case, since there is no direct subsidy attached to the program, most low-income families did not wish or could not afford to purchase a home, even on easy terms. Critics claim that the primary social impact of FHA insurance has been the financing of the movement of white middle-class families from the city to the suburb, thus creating the "white noose" around so many central city areas. Since 1968, when the economic soundness criteria was relaxed, FHA insurance has increasingly been available to low-income families. It has also been the mechanism through which the Section 235 and 236 programs, described later in this chapter have been financed.

[d]To some extent this increase was undoubtedly due to high mortgage interest rates and the difficulty of obtaining mortgage money in the non-subsidized sector that caused many builders to turn to the subsidized programs where money *was* available as a means of maintaining their production levels.

Table 3-2
Public Sector Housing Activity in Great Britain, 1966-1973

	Public Housing Starts (in Thousands)	Improvement Grants Approved
1966	186	117
1968	194	128
1969	177	124
1970	154	183
1971	137	236
1972	123	371
1973	112	453

Source: Data derived from U.K., Department of Environment, *Housing and Construction Statistics*, HMSO, No. 8, 4th Quarter, 1973, p. 23, 38-39, and U.K., Central Statistical Office, *Social Trends*, HMSO, No. 4, 1973, pp. 156, 158.

Table 3-3
U.S. Housing Starts, 1961-1973 (in Thousands)

	Federally Subsidized Starts (Including Public Housing)	Private Non-Subsidized Starts (Excluding Mobile Homes)	Subsidized Starts as Percent of Total
1961	36.2	1328.8	2.7
1965	63.7	1446.0	4.2
1966	70.9	1124.9	5.9
1967	91.4	1230.5	6.9
1968	165.5	1379.9	10.7
1969	199.9	1299.6	13.3
1970	429.8	1039.2	29.3
1971	430.0	1654.5	20.6
1972	338.8	2039.7	14.2
1973	181.1	1878.3	8.8

Source: U.S. Department of Housing and Urban Development, *Housing in the Seventies* (Washington, D.C.: HUD, 1973), p. 4-7.

Although the Democrats generally have given greater support to the concept of federal housing assistance for low- and moderate-income families, the table indicates that the really substantial increase in these programs came during Nixon's first term, after passage of the bipartisan Housing Act of 1968. Prior to that act the level of public sector activity was small and stable throughout the Eisenhower years (averaging 2.5 percent of all housing starts per year) when the only public sector activity was public housing, and then began to increase rapidly during the Kennedy and Johnson years (averaging 5 percent of total starts annually) with the advent of new Democratic programs.

In early 1973, however, President Nixon issued an order suspending most of the various federally assisted housing programs, pending an intensive evaluation of their performance and proposals for new legislation.[e] The effect of this suspension was to prevent the approval of any new federally assisted starts, but to allow applications already processed and approved to continue. As a result, federally assisted starts dropped substantially in 1973 to 8.8 percent of total starts, down from 14.2 percent of total starts the previous year, and this decline continued into 1974 as well. In the fall of 1973, President Nixon somewhat relaxed the suspension with respect to Section 23 public housing.[f] At that time the president indicated a desire to move from production-oriented subsidies to a consumer-oriented housing allowance program, pending a study of the latter's feasibility. At the present time, therefore, the public sector housing effort in the United States is in some confusion and disarray. However, it seems quite unlikely that public sector activity will ultimately diminish and retreat to the minor role it played prior to 1968, and in fact, the Housing and Community Development Act of 1974, signed into law by President Ford in August of that year, reinstituted the suspended programs, albeit on a reduced scale, and instituted a new Housing Assistance Program funded at $800 million for the first year (see Chapter 4, footnote h).

Finance

Each local housing authority in the United Kingdom maintains a Housing Revenue Account that, by statute, must not go into deficit. It accomplishes this feat through three sources of revenue: rents, rates (local property taxes), and subsidies from the central government. Since subsidies from the government are beyond the control of the local authority, prior to 1972 it was able to manipulate council housing rents and rates in order to meet its costs. The former imposed the burden upon the (relatively poorer) council tenant; the latter imposed the burden upon the (relatively more affluent) local taxpayer. (In the United Kingdom, rates are levied on the occupiers of property rather than the owners as in the United States, so the tax is structurally a consumption tax rather than a wealth tax.) Many local authorities were allowed to keep rents from soaring through use of a pooling arrangement by which the revenue in the

---

[e]The president cited the ineffectiveness of the programs in improving the housing conditions of low-income families, the high cost of the programs, and the red tape and complexity of the administrative apparatus as justification for the suspension.

[f]See the section on The Siting of Public Housing Labor in this chapter for an explanation of this program.

Housing Revenue Account could be applied to all units. Thus, the low cost of older units could be balanced off against the high cost of newer units, with the occupants of the former paying somewhat higher rents and occupants of the latter somewhat lower rents than would be required if each unit were to pay for itself.

Of total council housing income in 1971, rents accounted for about 70 percent, rates for another 10 percent, and central government subsidy for the remaining 20 percent.[g] However, as a result of the Housing Finance Act of 1972, the authority to set rents at the local authority's discretion was taken away, and all council house tenants must now pay a "fair rent" defined by national legislation. A new subsidy system, described below, protects the local Housing Revenue Account from deficit. However, the Labour Government has pledged itself to repeal of the 1972 Act and return to a financing system substantially similar to that which existed before 1972.

In the United States, local housing authorities receive revenues from only two sources: subsidies from the federal government and rents. Traditionally the federal subsidies have been (1) an annual payment sufficient to retire the bond issued by the local government to pay for the cost of construction, and (2) revenue lost to the federal government because interest income from local government bonds is exempt from federal income tax, which thus makes it much easier for local housing authorities to market large blocks of their bond issues to wealthy investors paying a high marginal tax rate. The only other revenue is from tenant rent, which is supposed to cover operating costs (including a payment by the local housing authority to the local government to partially compensate it for the fact that public housing is exempt from local property taxes). If rent is in excess of operating costs for a particular project, the resultant surplus cannot be pooled but must be returned to the federal government. Although this situation was frequent during the early years of public housing, the more recent situation is that rents are insufficient to cover operating costs. As a result, the federal government has recently had to initiate a new operating-cost subsidy to prevent local housing authorities from going bankrupt.

The only contribution made by local taxpayers is an invisible one through property tax revenue foregone because public housing is tax exempt. This payment—minus the amount received from the local housing authority as a partial payment in lieu of taxes—amounts to about 16 percent of the full cost of public housing. Although the U.S. local contribution thus somewhat exceeds that in the United Kingdom, it is a contribution in a form that is inflexible

---

[g]David Stafford, "Housing Policies," *Social and Economic Administration* 7, No. 2, May 1973, p. 116. Stafford points out, however, that these figures varied greatly from one local housing authority to another. Thus the average London borough rate contribution was 14.8 percent, with 55 percent of revenue coming from rents, while the average *small* rural district council contribution was less than 1 percent from rates and 73 percent from rents. See U.K., Department of Environment, *Housing and Construction Statistics*, No. 4, 4th Quarter, 1972, p. 68.

(there is no way for the local government to increase or decrease it) and that does not involve the local government in sharing any responsibility for the financial state of public housing within its boundaries. Given the relative unpopularity of public housing in the United States, this may well be the only means of extracting any financial contribution from fiscally hard-pressed American cities. Recent legislative proposals have suggested federal assistance to allow a substantial increase in the very modest payment to cities now made by local housing authorities in lieu of local property taxes.

Of total public housing revenues, rent accounts for 38 percent, and federal government subsidies make up the remaining 62 percent. Of total public housing costs (including the cost of tax-exempt U.S. securities and foregone local property tax), tenants contribute 26 percent through rent, the federal government pays 52 percent, and cities 16 percent.[5]

The United Kingdom has tried various subsidy mechanisms including requiring a specified local authority contribution per council house unit with a 100 percent subsidy by the national government above that level (not surprisingly that proved too costly); a set national subsidy per council house; and a subsidy designed to reduce local authority borrowing charges for council house building to 4 percent. Finally and currently, there exists a complicated set of subsidies by which (for the first time) rents must be set through nationally defined criteria ("fair rents") that require council house rents to be set on the same basis as rents in the private sector—a rent that the market would command assuming there were no excess of demand over supply in the area.[h] Any excess of expenditure over rent receipts is met through two subsidies (rising cost subsidy and operational deficit subsidy), each of which specifies the percent of the deficit that must be met through the rates and the percent that will be met by subsidy from the central government. The subsidies are set in such a way to eliminate any deficit in the Housing Revenue Account.

The Housing Act of 1972, which extended the fair-rent concept from the private to the public sector, was the subject of heated controversy. Prior to the act each local housing authority had been able to determine its own rent level for council housing units. These rent levels varied greatly from one local authority to another. In 1971, the year before the Housing Finance Act went into effect, the average weekly council house rent varied among local authorities from a high of £3.88 to a low of £1.35.[i]

However, these variations were not necessarily related to need. Residents of council housing in some areas (those where large numbers of units had been built many years ago at very little cost) were able to gain the benefit of low rents through the pooling process described above. By using the lower cost of older units to offset the much higher cost of newer units, rents could be maintained at a relatively low level throughout the area.[j] In many cases, however, areas with

---

[h]See Chapter 4 for an explanation of how fair rents are determined.
[i]National Association of Local Governmental Officials, *The Way Ahead*, London, 1973, pp. 60-66. These figures are exclusive of rates.
[j]Thus the older units were charged a somewhat higher rent than was necessary solely to cover their costs.

the most pressing needs were those with a high proportion of new to old housing, and in these areas, council housing rents were much higher.

Furthermore, central government subsidies were based not on need or the state of the Housing Revenue Account, but on per unit subsidies that varied according to the legislation in force at the time the unit was constructed. Finally, because of the pooling arrangement and the per unit subsidy, council house rents were often lower than the fair rents charged for comparable private, unfurnished rental units after 1965.

In 1971, the average council house unrebated rent in Greater London was £3.48 per week while the average privately rented unfurnished unit was £6.20 per week. In the rest of England and Wales, the figures were £2.35 and £3.70, respectively.[k]

The Conservative Government argued strongly in terms quite similar to those used by President Nixon, when he suspended U.S. federal housing programs in 1973, that this situation was both inequitable and expensive. In response, legislation was passed that required council house rents be set according to the same criteria as private sector rents. Thus local authorities would set a fair rent based on the characteristics and location of the unit and assign a market value that did not include a scarcity value. Appeals could be made to local rent scrutiny boards. Under the fair-rent clause, public and private sector housing of the same quality and standard would charge similar rents, and public sector housing of the same quality and standard but in different local authorities would also charge similar rents. Since this would mean a rent increase for most council house residents, the increases were to be introduced in stages. Parallel with the introduction of fair rents, the government also introduced a rent-rebate and allowance scheme for households with high rents relative to their income. Together the schemes covered both the public and private rental sector (see Chapter 6).

This legislation met with strong opposition; several local authorities implemented it only after threat of court orders. The Labour Party pledged to overturn this act, and one of its first decisions upon taking office in early 1974 was to announce a rent freeze on all housing, including council housing. Although one might expect dislike of a measure that both raised rents for many people and simultaneously took future rent decisions out of the hands of locally elected officials,[l] much of the opposition apparently resulted from the clash between the pursuit of the abstract principle of equity and established social service objectives.

---

[k]U.K., Central Statistical Office, *Social Trends*, HMSO, No. 4, 1973, p. 163. These figures are exclusive of rates.

[l]During the first year's operation of the act, council house *unrebated* rents indeed increased sharply, particularly outside the Greater London area. In the year prior to the act's passage (April 1971 to April 1972), unrebated rents rose 10 percent there, and 5 percent in Greater London. After passage of the act, the respective annual increases were 27 percent and 19 percent (April 1972 to May 1973). However, *rebated* rent (the rent tenants actually pay after they receive their rent rebate and supplementary benefit, if any, increased by only 16 percent outside Greater London and 11 percent in Greater London during the same time. This represents an increase over the 10 percent and 7 percent rates by which rebated rents rose in the year prior to passage of the act, but an increase markedly less than that in unrebated rents.

Many people viewed low council house rents as one of the social service advantages provided by public sector housing. Now it was to be abandoned for the sake of an abstract equity. As Anthony Crosland, Labour spokesman for Housing, wrote:

I believe there are overwhelming objections to the principle of so-called "fair rents" in the public sector. First the proposal has no logic. The Government are fond of pointing to Labour's 1965 Act and arguing that if "fair rents" are right for the private rented sector then logically they must be right for the public rented sector. This is not so.

Fair rents in the private sector are designed to give the landlord a reasonable profit to provide for good maintenance and improvement while eliminating scarcity values in places like London. But there is no parallel requirement in the public sector, which has a large and varied stock of housing of different dates over which it can spread the costs of maintenance and improvement.[6]

In short, fair rents, it was argued, produced a "profit" for council housing. To many people, particularly Labour Party adherents, this was an example of the pursuit of "profits"—that is, a surplus in the public sector—driving out important social objectives. To others, it enhanced equity by eliminating irrational discrepancies among local authorities with respect to council rents and between rents in the public and private housing sectors.

The two new central government subsidies designed to supplement fair rent as local housing authority revenue were based on the state of the Housing Revenue Account after the collection of fair rent. The new system had the virtue of being tied to increases in local housing authority expenditure whether through new building, maintenance, repair or improved services, insofar as these additional expenditures were not met by increases in rental income. The subsidy is divided by a predetermined formula between local authority and national government with the former contributing 25 percent through rates, and the latter bearing the remaining 75 percent.

As has already been noted, in the United States, the federal government subsidy has been until very recently tied solely to the capital cost of construction. Operating costs therefore had to be financed completely through rent charges, since, except for minor exceptions, there is no recourse to local financial resources. Local housing authorities have quite predictably reacted by attempting to reduce operating and maintenance costs (including social services, police protection, and so forth) to a minimum and by raising rent to relatively high levels, albeit levels constrained by statute. The latter stratagem has resulted in public housing in some areas being occupied not predominantly by those who are literally destitute and thus worst off, but by those who, while very poor, nonetheless have at least some income—if only in the form of public assistance payments.

However, soaring operating costs and lower revenues—caused by a new federal law limiting rent to 25 percent of an occupant's income—finally forced the federal government to initiate a subsidy to help offset operating costs. This subsidy began in 1970 and amounted to $31 million that year. It rose quickly to $280 million in 1973, and the Nixon Administration, forseeing an ever-increasing burden on the federal budget through uncontrolled increases in operating costs, attempted to maintain payments at that level by refusing to spend any more even though Congress made additional funds available. The administration feared that since no local contribution was required, housing authorities had no incentive to control cost and would "irresponsibly" increase spending with the expectation of being bailed out by the federal government. Although this fear appears somewhat exaggerated in the context of very real needs for improving maintenance and service on the part of most housing authorities, it does seem reasonable to require some local contribution, particularly since the federal government through revenue sharing is now contributing substantial sums to local governments to be used as these governments see fit rather than for specifically designated purposes as federal grants-in-aid traditionally have been.

**Public Housing as a Social Service—
Tenant Selection and Characteristics**

In the United Kingdom, selection of tenants is at the discretion of the local authority, although national legislation enacted in 1957 specifies that the first priority must be given to those displaced through clearance schemes and then, more generally, to persons presently occupying unsanitary or overcrowded housing, having large families, or living under unsatisfactory housing conditions. Until 1949, council housing was defined by legislation as "working-class" housing, and restricted to members of the working class.[m] However, that restriction has been removed, and there are now no specific eligibility criteria limiting residence in public sector housing. Philosophically the predominant view of council housing is as a universalist social service rather than a selective program for the needy. Thus, when or where there has been an adequate supply of council units, the result has been some degree of socioeconomic mix that, in any case, is viewed as a good in itself by many.

Unfortunately in a situation of shortage, some form of selection criterion must be resorted to. In many inner-city areas, the amount of available council housing is insufficient to rehouse the homeless or those displaced through clearance programs (who are not necessarily in the low-income category), which groups generally have first claim on empty council units. Long waiting lists are not unusual and it may be years after initial application before a family that has *not* been displaced may finally receive a council unit. In some cases—generally where there is no shortage of council units—an applicant's position on the waiting list is determined simply by date of application; in other local authorities

---
[m]However, a specific income level was never tied to that definition.

position is determined through a point scheme or a merit scheme based on relative housing need, which criterion is not necessarily coincidental with low income. However, even in these latter schemes, length of time on the waiting list is normally considered a form of need in itself and is awarded substantial points.[n]

The result of more than fifty years of council house building and tenant selection policy in the United Kingdom is that while council housing is predominantly working class (and is certainly perceived to be so, probably more than it actually is), nevertheless the socioeconomic diversity of council housing tenants is substantial particularly when compared to the United States. This results in a considerable tension between, on the one hand, the strongly held view that, conceptually, council housing should be a universalist social service and that council housing should represent a social-economic mix and, on the other hand, the apparently equally strongly held view that the neediest should be helped first. Much criticism is directed toward the local authorities for their inability to house many in severe needs. Yet, within the context of a shortage of council housing units relative to demand, it is difficult to see how this could be accomplished without what, for all practical purposes, would be income limitations for entrance and perhaps on continued residence as well.

In the United States, admission to public housing is indeed limited in just this way. To qualify for public housing, households must have an income below a "typically low annual wage" in the area. In general, this is interpreted to mean an annual income less than five times that of the rental charged for the lowest cost private housing available in substantial supply and inhabited by blue-collar workers. This level varies, however, with family size. Table 3-4 lists income limits

Table 3-4
Income Limits for U.S. Public Housing for a Family of Four, 1972

New York City	$7,800
Chicago	6,500
Los Angeles	6,100
Boston	6,000
Washington, D.C.	5,800
Kansas City	5,500
Atlanta	5,000
Philadelphia	4,800

Source: U.S., Department of Housing and Urban Development, *Housing in the Seventies* (Washington, D.C.: HUD, 1973), p. 1-45.

---

[n]For a description and analysis of the various selection schemes, see U.K., Ministry of Housing and Local Government, *Council Housing Purposes, Priorities and Procedures*, HMSO, 1969, ch. 3.

in 1972 for eligibility for a family of four in several different American cities. (The median income for such a family in 1972 was $10,532.)

In most cities residents must leave public housing if their income rises to exceed the maximum limit for admission by more than 25 percent. It is obvious that this regulation (which, of course, has no counterpart in the United Kingdom) is vicious and detrimental both to the families evicted—not only because they are uprooted but because it is difficult for them to find equivalent private sector housing without a substantial rent increase—and to the public housing program for it systematically rids itself of its most stable and successful tenants. The persistence of this perverse regulation,[o] despite years of bitter criticism, is surely a testament to the degree to which Americans believe that public housing should be housing for the poor. This belief appears to be shared by conservatives, who emphasize individual initiative and private market solutions for all but those unable to purchase such a solution, and by "liberals," who believe that those most in need (i.e., the poor) should be first served by enlightened government social policy.[p]

The result of these income limitations is a distribution of residents in public housing focused almost completely on the low end of the income scale. Table 3-5 compares the distribution of public housing residents by income class in the United States and the United Kingdom in 1972, when median income for all households was $9,225 in the United States and £2,025 in the United Kingdom.

As Table 3-5 indicates, more than 75 percent of public housing households in the United States have incomes less than half of U.S. median household income, while only 26.3 percent of council housing households in the United Kingdom have income less than half of U.K. median income. Fully 40 percent of households residing in council dwellings have incomes higher than the national median income in the United Kingdom; in the United States, the parallel figure is less than one-half of one percent.

The lack of income limitation allows, but does not fully account for, the much greater income diversity of residents in council housing in the United Kingdom compared to public housing in the United States. Other causal factors undoubtedly include the relatively greater stigma associated with public housing residence in the United States; the perception in the United States, not altogether untrue, that public housing is a breeding ground for crime, drug addiction, and despair; the confinement of most public housing to the poorest and most deteriorating central city neighborhoods; the quality of council housing that is much better, relative to the private sector, in the United Kingdom than it is in the United States; and the greater availability of private sector rental housing in the United States than in the United Kingdom.

---

[o]It was finally repealed in the Housing and Community Development Act of 1974.

[p]In addition to income limitations, U.S. federal legislation, until passage of the Housing Act of 1974, prohibited local housing authorities from setting rents at a level exceeding 80 percent of the lowest rent for which a substantial volume of standard housing is available on the private market.

Table 3-5
Public Housing Households in the United States and the United Kingdom, by Income Distribution, 1972

Gross Household Income as a Percent of Gross Median Income	Percent of Total Households Residing in Public Housing U.K.	U.S.
Less than 25% of median	8.1	36.5
Between 25-50% of median	18.2	40.6
Between 50-75% of median	15.6	15.4
Between 75-100% of median	17.8	7.0
Between 100-125% of median	14.7	.5
Between 125-150% of median	10.3	–
Between 150-200% of median	10.1	–
More than 200% of median	5	–

The above table is derived from the following two tables.

United Kingdom		United States	
Gross Weekly Household Income (£)	Percent of All Council Households	Gross Annual Household Income ($)	Percent of All Public Housing Households
Under £10	8.3	0- 999	2.4
10-15	11.3	100-1999	26.8
15-20	7.4	2000-2999	23.5
20-25	7.7	3000-3999	17.3
25-30	8.4	4000-4999	11.7
30-35	8.5	5000-5999	4.9
35-40	10.0	6000-6999	4.3
40-45	7.5	7000-7999	2.6
45-50	7.1	More than 8000	4.0
50-60	10.0		
60-80	9.6		
Over 80	4.0		

Source: U.K. data is derived from U.K., Department of Employment, *Family Expenditure Survey Report for 1972*, HMSO, 1973, pp. 14-15. U.S. data is derived from U.S., Department of Housing and Urban Development, *Housing in the Seventies* (Washington, D.C.: HUD, 1973), p. 4-91.

The effects of this concentration of low-income people in U.S. public housing are perhaps inseparable from their causes. Public housing is stigmatized as "poor peoples' housing." It is also increasingly perceived as "black peoples' housing." Partly because a disproportionate portion of the poor are black (31.3 percent) and partly because public housing is disproportionately located where blacks reside, public housing *is* disproportionately black occupied. About 70 percent of all public housing residents are black compared to only 12 percent of the entire U.S. population. Public housing also tends to attract those families who have the fewest options in the private market—large families and/or female-headed families with very low incomes. In short, public housing has a disproportionate share of problem families who both require more intensive assistance and generate more negative externalities (crime, vandalism, and so forth) for their fellow tenants. Unlike council housing in the United Kingdom, which is housing predominantly for the working class and encompasses a social-economic mix, public housing in the United States is housing for the very poor and problem families—the subworking class. Thus, nearly 40 percent of all households in public housing with family heads under 65 have no wage earners in the labor force; all income for these households derives from public transfer payments.[7]

The Siting of Public Housing

For all these reasons (class, race, crime, and so forth) the introduction of public housing projects (except those for the elderly) into stable, working-class or middle-class neighborhoods in the United States is vigorously, and often successfully, opposed by existing residents. There is, it is true, somewhat less opposition to decentralized scattered-site public housing than to high-rise projects, and, indeed, an increasing number of units added to the public housing stock are low-rise and scattered. (Many of these units have "entered the stock" through Section 23 of the 1965 Housing Act in which the public housing agency rents existing private units at market rents, then manages the units and sublets them at below market rents to tenants eligible for public housing.)[q] There is clearly much *less* opposition to public housing projects for the elderly. The elderly are not perceived to "cause problems" themselves or as having children who "cause problems." During recent years, more than 40 percent of newly built public housing units have been designed for occupation by the elderly. This suggests current American opposition to public housing may be due more to dislike and fear of its residents than to ideological strictures against public sector ownership.

Even though council housing in the United Kingdom does not suffer from the same sort of problems due to the characteristics of its residents as does public housing in the United States, it nonetheless suffers from some of the same problems of neighborhood opposition. In London, primary responsibility for

---

[q]Nearly 25 percent of all units added to the stock of public housing since 1965 have been Section 23 units and the Housing Act of 1970 required 30 percent of all future units added be of this type. Section 23 was the one program retained by President Nixon after his suspension of federally assisted programs. See Frank De Leeuw and Sam H. Leaman, "The Section 23 Program," U.S. Joint Economic Committee, *The Economics of Federal Subsidy Programs*, Part 5, GPO, 1972, pp. 642-59.

building and administering council housing rests with the 32 separate boroughs. Most of these boroughs' local housing authorities have residence requirements for admission to either or both the waiting list and council housing itself. The effect of this is to greatly inhibit mobility and to ensure that the need for council housing in the more affluent outer boroughs is kept to a minimum. Most of the authorities in the outer boroughs appear willing to build sufficient council housing to meet the needs of their own present residents—but they have no desire to house presently ill-housed inner borough residents. This is particularly so for outer boroughs with Conservative councils that might not wish to encourage Labour voters to immigrate. Greater London Council (GLC) does have "overspill" power to build housing in any borough, if it can obtain the land to do so. It also can arrange negotiated agreements whereby outer boroughs agree to offer some of their available council units to households living in an inner borough and presently on the inner borough's waiting list. However, in the latter case, success is totally dependent on the good will of the outer borough, and this has not been readily forthcoming. In the former case, local boroughs have, in effect, a veto over GLC's land acquisition efforts, and the outer boroughs have not hesitated to use this. (The central government, in turn, has a veto over this veto, but the Conservative Government in power from 1970 to 1974 was very reluctant to use it. The Labour Government elected in the spring of 1974 has promised to be more aggressive in this respect.) As a result, the majority of the ill-housed in London and other major conurbations are in the inner city, while the solutions to their problems remain out of reach in the outer boroughs where land for housebuilding is more readily available.

In the United States, much the same situation occurs with respect to central city and suburbs. The local housing authority generally coincides with the city boundaries (which at least allows more mobility and scope for decision making than in the United Kingdom), but the suburbs—where job opportunities are increasingly located—are outside of the LHA's jurisdiction. And unlike London, with rare exceptions, there are no mechanisms available for overruling a suburb's decision not to allow public housing.

The fact that London faces difficulties similar in this respect to those faced by American cities—even though conditions would appear much more favorable for suburban acceptance of public sector housing since race is not a major factor—surely ought to serve as a warning about how difficult and intractable the problem may be in the United States. At least in London, however, there appears to be little opposition to providing adequate council housing for present borough residents (although resource constraints may prevent it), which situation is not true in most suburbs of American cities.

Quasi-Public Sector Housing

To give a complete picture, it should also be mentioned that several other U.S. housing programs have performed a social service function similar to that of public housing. These are programs that provide substantial, direct federal subsidies for housing in the private sector, both rental and home ownership. In total, these programs accounted for 1.8 percent of all dwelling units as of 1972, although they accounted for a much higher portion of new units added to the stock from 1969 to 1972. These programs provide subsidies attached to the capital cost of the dwelling. On the homeownership side, the subsidy can—depending on the purchaser's income—reduce his mortgage repayments to the level he would pay if his mortgage were bearing an interest of only 1 percent. The purchaser obtains an FHA-insured mortgage on the private market (usually at an interest rate slightly lower than non-FHA-insured mortgages) and HUD makes up the difference between the FHA-insured mortgage interest rate and the same principal with a 1 percent interest rate. On the rental side, non-profit, limited dividend or cooperative sponsors receive a similar subsidy in return for which they agree to rent their premises at a rate that reflects their subsidized mortgage cost—generally at a level low enough for low- and moderate-income families to afford. In both homeownership and rental cases, the resident must contribute a set portion of his income (20 percent in the former case, 25 percent in the latter) towards the cost, and the government pays the remainder up to the maximum subsidy level.

There are some advantages in these approaches compared to public housing. Income limitations are much higher than public housing (generally up to 80 percent of median income in an area), and residents do not have to move if their income rises to a level above the eligibility line. In most cases, the initiative rests not with the city government but with the private developer, who in response to the profit motive, has proven much more enthusiastic about building housing for low-income people than have local governments, most of which, in response to public opinion, have been resistant. (Indeed city governments or local housing authorities are largely uninvolved in these interest subsidy programs—the subsidy goes directly to the private developer, and the unit is sold, rented, and managed almost as though it were private housing.) Eligibility checks on prospective tenants and home purchasers are conducted not by the city's local housing authority, but by HUD's regional and area offices. The only power that city governments have over these programs is through their power to zone land in such a way to prevent the building of low-income housing (e.g., minimum acreage requirements, restrictions on multi-family residences, and so forth).

High-rise projects have been avoided, and, in fact, the housing that has been built through such programs is unlabelled and usually indistinguishable from private housing, which has thus greatly lessened the stigma effect. Because of the lower concentration of units relative to public housing, some of the more deleterious externalities on the neighborhood environment have been avoided.

There are, unfortunately, corresponding disadvantages. Because the subsidy is attached to the capital cost of construction, the homeowner or tenant must bear the full burden of increases in operating costs and local property taxes (and both have spiralled); because the city and LHA are largely uninvolved, there is a lack of coordination and, indeed, of interest on their parts; because the subsidy operates primarily through the private sector with no local participation and relatively little federal oversight, caveat emptor has been its operative philosophy to the frequent detriment of low-income and poorly educated home buyers and to the great advantage of many home builders, realtors, and property managers; and because most of the housing is new, the program has generated much jealousy and political opposition from lower-middle- and middle-income households that are just above the maximum income level and therefore ineligible for the program but nonetheless cannot afford new or equivalent housing in the private unsubsidized market. It is this last "disadvantage" that may be the most important in determining the future of these programs. The severity and social divisiveness of this equity problem is illustrated by this letter from a constituent to his Congressman:

As a member of the usually silent majority and an ardent supporter of yours I believe that I should bring to your attention some things that, from my point of view, should be corrected. First of all, I am a young man of 25 employed as the personnel supervisor of a growing concern in the area where my wife is also employed. Between us we earn approximately eleven thousand dollars per year and live within our means in a modest three-room apartment in a 40-year-old building. A new (subsidized) housing area . . . is now open for tenants who earn less than six thousand per annum. These apartments are as large or larger than ours and in beautiful condition, and the rent is actually less than I am paying. Is it possible that this situation can be justified?[8]

Within the British context, these U.S. programs involving direct federal subsidies but no public ownership bear some similarity to the legally non-profit voluntary housing associations and housing societies. The housing associations build, acquire, improve, and manage housing to rent, often in close cooperation with local authorities. Prior to 1972, they were eligible for 100 percent loans at low interest rates from local authorities and, at the local authority's discretion, any per unit subsidy provided by the central government.

Since the Housing Finance Act of 1972, housing association units are covered by fair rent legislation, tenants are eligible for rent allowances, and government subsidies cover deficits in the same way as they do for local authorities. New housing association units are eligible for 100 percent loans if they make 50 percent of their units available for households selected by the local authority from their waiting list. And, for the first time, housing associations are eligible for loans from the Housing Corporation, a government body capitalized with public funds and set up in 1964 to help promote housing societies.[r]

Housing societies in contrast with housing associations, build for cost-rent and co-ownership. They have not received direct government subsidies although

---

[r]Legislation under consideration at the time of writing would further expand the powers of the Housing Corporation to promote and regulate housing associations.

the Housing Corporation may provide up to one-third of their mortgage financing. The remaining two-thirds must come from conventional sources, usually building societies.

In aggregate, voluntary housing associations and societies account for about 1.5 percent of the U.K. housing stock,[9] and about 2.8 percent of all new completions between 1970 and 1972.[10] The great majority of these are housing association units.

As the private rental sector continues to decline (see Chapter 4) the voluntary housing movement is looked upon by some as an important means of retaining choice and diversity in an increasingly local authority-dominated rental sector. Thus, the Conservative Government White Paper, *Widening the Choice: the Next Steps in Housing* stated:

Many people prefer to rent their home or cannot afford to buy it. They too must have an adequate choice of decent accommodation. But for them, the choice is becoming increasingly narrow. The private rental sector continues to decline. The Government believes that the trend towards a municipal monopoly of rented accommodation is unhealthy in itself. . . . The government therefore proposes to widen the range and choice of rented accommodation by the expansion of the voluntary housing movement.[11]

And at least a portion of the Labour Party appears to agree, as evidenced by comments made by the Secretary of State for the Environment, Anthony Crosland shortly after the Labour Government came to power in early 1974:

I have always been a firm supporter of the voluntary housing movement—more so, perhaps, than some people in my own party. I believe it would be intolerable if we ever reached a situation in which only two forms of housing were available in this country—in which everyone either had to become a tenant of a local authority or had to buy his own home. Monopoly is as undesirable in housing as it is elsewhere.[12]

Legislation introduced by the Conservative Government in 1973 designed to strengthen the voluntary housing movement was reintroduced nearly without change by the Labour Government when it took office in 1974.

Summary and Conclusion

Public sector housing in the U.K. represents nearly one-third of the housing stock compared to less than 2 percent in the United States. Its residents comprise a far greater social-economic mix than do residents of U.S. public housing. It therefore is not surprising that the problems each country faces in this sector bear little relation to each other.

American problems are focused on how to house and provide services to large numbers of very poor families with a multitude of problems, and how to cope with crime, vandalism, and resultant high operating and maintenance costs. These problems are not absent in the United Kingdom—in fact, many point to several council housing estates in Glasgow as suffering from much the same syndrome—but they are certainly much less common and dominant. Instead council housing problems in the United Kingdom are related to shortage of housing accommodation, particularly in London and other large urban centers. The demand for council dwelling units in these areas far outstrips supply.

From a longer-range perspective, the United Kingdom must cope with a series of problems arising from the sheer size of the public sector. A dominant public sector may not necessarily imply a lack of choice and diversity, population immobility, and large and cumbersome bureaucracies with little responsiveness to human needs. But if these conditions are to be avoided, considerably more thought and effort will have to be devoted to how to do so than has been the case so far.

4
Private Rental Housing

Although the private rental sector is quite substantial in the United States and quite small in the United Kingdom, it is in this area that both countries experience their most severe housing problems. The United Kingdom has been considerably more willing than the United States to adopt a social service approach with respect to residents in the private rental sector and to intervene in an effort to improve the situation.

Historically the two main British responses have been rent control, which we consider in this chapter, and security of tenure, which we examine more closely in the next. These responses, while they have been mostly successful within their own framework of objectives, have nonetheless not solved the problems of the private rental sector in the United Kingdom. Instead, the nature of these problems has now changed—some would say as a result of efforts to solve them through rent control and security of tenure. The present problem is that the private rental sector in the United Kingdom has simply ceased, on the whole, to be able to yield a reasonable return on investment and has become economically non-viable. The same condition—albeit for different reasons—appears to be enveloping the low-income sector of the private rental market in U.S. urban centers. Both countries are struggling to devise appropriate social service responses to cope with these deteriorating situations.

In this chapter, we assess the impact of rent control, examine the size, scope, and condition of the private residential rental sector, and the reasons for its decline; we also look at remedies that have been proposed.

Rent Control

In Chapter 2, we defined a social service policy as one in which the government accepted responsibility for assuring not only that all its citizens are decently housed, but also that they are housed at a price within their means. The price one can "afford" for housing is, of course, a relative concept. In the United States, it is generally thought that housing should not account for more than 25 percent of personal income, while in the United Kingdom, housing cost-income ratio expectations have been substantially below this, perhaps at the level of 10 to 15 percent. (The actual ratio has, in fact, been rising rapidly—far more rapidly than expectations.)

Clearly an absolute shortage of units will force prices up beyond these levels for many people. Such an absolute shortage has, until recently, chronically characterized housing in the United Kingdom, but not the United States. While the United Kingdom now has a nationwide surplus of units over households, shortages still exist in some critical areas, particularly the London region. However, even when there is no actual shortage of housing, the real cost of providing a dwelling unit (assuming a normal return and not exorbitant profits) is so high that in both countries many lower-income people will have great difficulty obtaining standard housing within their means.

The United Kingdom has reacted to this by introducing a series of rent-control measures for the private rental sector. First introduced in 1915 as a temporary wartime measure, rent control in one form or another has been a permanent fixture of the British life ever since. Nonetheless, throughout most of its history, many experts, observers, and public officials have viewed it as a necessary evil to be maintained only for as long as a severe housing shortage persisted.

During the past two decades, however, it appears to have become accepted, in one form or another, as a permanent feature of the British social service tradition. In this, it reflects the minority view of an early Commission of Inquiry into rent control—the 1937 Ridley Commission—that housing is "a social service of such extreme importance [that it] ought to be controlled, the public being protected against extortion and improper treatment." As Cullingworth comments, "on this view, control should be regarded not as a temporary expedient, but as a permanent and desirable feature of 'the housing service'."[1]

In the United States, rent control traditionally has not been considered an appropriate device, partly for ideological reasons and partly due to the widespread belief that it would not work, that the end result of rent control would be a worsening of the housing situation for many people. However, rent control was invoked on a nationwide basis as an emergency measure during World War II and also during Phases I and II of President Nixon's economic stabilization policy in 1971-72. (It was revoked during Phase III and not renewed during Phase IV.) New York City has had rent-control legislation continually since the World War II imposed measure that it chose not to remove. New York is the only major American city with substantial experience with rent control. Recently several city and county governments have given serious consideration to rent-control ordinances in response to soaring rents, and some, including Boston, Cambridge, Massachusetts, and Washington, D.C., have actually passed them.

The effects of rent control may vary considerably with the structure of the system imposed. British rent control, when first introduced in 1915, simply froze all rents at pre-1915 levels. This was later modified to allow up to a 40 percent increase over prewar rents. In 1923 rent control was shifted from the unit to the tenant, so that rents would be freed if a sitting tenant voluntarily moved (necessitating further legislation to assure tenants some security of tenure so that their landlords could not evict them as a means of raising rents.)

Legislation in 1933 and 1938 also contributed to progressively decontrolling rents. However, the advent of the Second World War called forth a new freeze of all rents at 1939 levels. This remained in force until the early 1950s when the Conservative Government permitted rents to increase by an amount necessary to repair and maintain structures to 1939 standards. In 1957, rents on housing with relatively high gross values[a] were decontrolled upon their vacancy by the Tories. The Rent Act of 1965, passed by the Labour Government, did not reimpose rent control on decontrolled units, but substituted a (somewhat) more flexible system of rent regulation based on a "fair-rent" concept. The 1972 Act extended rent regulation to those unfurnished units still covered by rent control. However, when the new Labour Government took office in early 1974, one of its first acts was to impose an across the board freeze on all rents. It did this administratively and presumably as an emergency measure.

Thus, under existing legislation, all unfurnished private tenancies except luxury ones are covered by rent-regulation legislation. Rents are frozen at their 1965 level until a "fair rent" is registered by a rent officer upon application by either landlord or tenant, or both jointly. Most applications have been initiated by landlords and most (87 percent of the total in 1972) have resulted in rent increases. It is ironic—though understandable given the price increases since the fair-rent legislation passed in 1965—that fair rents, initially passed primarily to regain some measure of control over the rents of tenancies decontrolled by the 1957 Rent Act, should have resulted in higher rents. Indeed, in 1966, the first year of fair rents, most requests for determination were from tenants and more decisions (57 percent)[2] resulted in rent decreases. The explanation appears to be that the act froze the rents of covered tenancies at 1965 levels until they were registered at which point they received fair rents and clearly prices as a whole have risen considerably over the 1965 levels at which the rents were frozen.

What is a fair rent? The legislation specifies that it is to be determined for a dwelling unit by taking into account all the circumstances of the unit (other than the personal circumstances of the owner and occupier), in particular its age, character, locality, and state of repair. It is not, however, to include scarcity value; fair rent is to be calculated under the assumption that the number of tenants seeking a dwelling of that type (assuming rent level is not a factor) will not exceed supply. Assuming this is possible (and since housing is a very differentiated good, it is hard to conceive of a situation where every differentiable set of units had exactly the same number of potential buyers as there were dwellings in that set), the equilibrium price would simply be the cost of supplying the unit, including an opportunity cost providing a reasonable return on investment.

However, it is apparent that the above explanation is not what "fair rent"

---

[a]Gross value is an appraisers term referring to the rent a property would command, assuming the tenant paid rates and utilities and the landlord bore the cost of repairs, insurance and other expenses. The gross value, however, must be "reasonable"—that is, not inflated by conditions of scarcity.

envisions. As Della Nevitt points out: "This ['fair rent'] is a valuers' concept which presupposes the possibility of removing the scarcity element, and setting a 'fair' rent which is a rent or price that owes much to the old metaphysical discussions on the 'just' price and nothing at all to modern economics. It is a dangerous concept to have introduced into a twentieth-century Act and has inevitably created much debate and some ill-feeling. The concept may, however, be retained for many years because any form of rent regulation seems preferable to arbitrary eviction and/or increases in rent."[3] The effect of "fair rents" is that all private sector unfurnished rents are set by negotiation and arbitration among landlord, tenant, and rent officer; the rents can be renegotiated after three years. Provision is made for appeal to part-time local rent assessment committees that are set up specifically for these purposes.

Furnished tenancies, which, particularly in London, tend to house the most disadvantaged segments of the population, are not subject to this form of rent regulation or control, although a tenant may make application to the Furnished Houses Rent Tribunal for a "reasonable" rent. However, furnished tenants, unlike their counterparts in unfurnished accommodation, do not have security of tenure. Efforts to achieve rent reduction through the Rent Tribunal procedure may result in a lower rent followed shortly thereafter by eviction.

As a result of the rent regulation of unfurnished tenancies, owners of these properties have a strong incentive to either sell when they are able to (see Chapter 5) either for owner-occupancy or for conversion to luxury flats with uncontrolled rents or to convert flats to furnished properties. The Francis Committee, appointed by the same Labour Government that introduced rent regulation in 1965, concluded:

The present position is that, on the one hand there is little incentive for landlords to let saleable units of accomodation as compared with selling them, and on the other hand there is a strong awareness on the part of that section of the public which is able to buy a house or a flat of the advantages, in times of high taxation and inflation, of purchasing one's home. This option, however, is not open to the low wage earners and to other categories of persons in low-income groups. The tragedy of the present situation is that so little private accommodation is available for letting unfurnished to that class of persons, at any rate in the stress areas. The other side of the picture is this. The only sector of the private housing market which has shown some sign of buoyancy in recent years is the furnished sector. There can be little doubt that there has been a significant "switch" on the part of landlords from letting unfurnished to letting furnished.[4]

Between 1963 and 1969, the portion of rented accomodation in the furnished sector in London increased from 18 percent to 24 percent of all rented units,[5] and the amount of unfurnished accomodation coming vacant and up for reletting dropped precipitously relative to furnished. In comparable five-week periods in 1963 and 1970, the London Weekly Advertiser carried the following number of advertisements for rental of flats and houses.[6]

Furnished		Unfurnished	
1963	1970	1963	1970
855	1,290	340	42

In the United States, municipal experience with rent control has, for all practical purposes been limited to New York City. There, most private rental units in multiple dwelling buildings built before 1946 are subject to rent control. Rent ceilings are based on rents charged in 1943 with one across-the-board 15 percent increase granted in 1953. The landlord can pass along to the tenant in increased rent any direct labor cost increases for building services. He may pass along increases for additional building services or new equipment only with the tenant's consent, or in the case of improvements affecting the entire building, only with the consent of one-half to three-fourths of the building's tenants, depending on the improvement. When a voluntary vacancy occurs, the landlord can increase rent by 15 percent, but he cannot do this more than once every two years. In addition, the landlord can qualify for increased rent under a hardship provision providing he has no outstanding housing code violations. If the landlord does not provide a level of building maintenance and services equivalent to that provided in 1943, tenants may apply for a rent reduction. In 1968, there were 350,000 such applications for reduction, of which 57,000 were granted. The average reduction granted was $11 per month.[7]

Rent control was originally not imposed on post-1947 units for fear of discouraging new investment in the rental market. However, in 1969 a more flexible rent stabilization policy was imposed on most post-1947 units.

Although rent control would seem to be anathema to the American free-market ideology, the federally subsidized rent control programs discussed in Chapter 3 incorporate a rent-control mechanism. In return for receiving a subsidy tied to capital costs, the owner signs an agreement with HUD to charge a basic rent that covers amortization based on a 1 percent loan, operating costs, taxes, and (in the case of limited dividend sponsor) a return on investment of no more than 6 percent. The tenant must then pay the basic rent or 25 percent of income, whichever is greater. Any excess paid over the basic rent, however, must be turned over to HUD. The basic rent cannot be increased without HUD's approval, though normally it is increased to allow for increases in operating costs and taxes.

The rationale for rent control is clearly to provide a social service to housing consumers by enabling them to occupy housing of a given standard at a lower cost to them than they would have to bear at market prices for such a unit. How well has this succeeded? In their study of the demand for rental housing in New York, the Rand Institute first developed a regression equation to explain the rent of uncontrolled dwelling units, then used the equation (whose independent variables included location, age, condition of structure, number of rooms, and so forth) to predict market rents for controlled dwelling units. The results showed that the median difference between estimated market rent for a unit and its actual controlled rent was $48 per month and the mean difference was $54 per month. They concluded that "our analysis supports the general belief that in 1968 controlled housing was a substantial bargain for its tenants."[8]

However, the quality of dwelling units under rent control was not only substantially lower than uncontrolled units whose rent was the same as the estimated market rent of the controlled units, it was also lower than uncontrolled units whose market rent was equal to the controlled rent. The study found:

At any given rent per room controlled housing seems to be in worse condition than uncontrolled housing. . . . At rents under $15 per room 48.7 percent of the controlled units and 70 percent of the uncontrolled units were in buildings classified as "sound" by the fieldworkers of the 1968 Housing and Vacancy Survey. Even at rents of $50 or more per room, the incidence of substandard buildings was higher in the controlled inventory. In these terms controlled housing seems to be no bargain, but a worse buy than uncontrolled housing.[b]

Rent control and regulation in the United Kingdom likewise has undoubtedly resulted in rents lower than market levels. In 1969, of those units in Greater London switching to fair rent (defined as market value less the scarcity factor) the average previous rent was £190 per annum, while the average fair rent registered for the dwelling was £270. And, since there is a severe housing shortage in London, fair rent, by definition, is still less than market rent. The Francis Committee concluded that nationally fair rents were below market rent by an average of about 20 percent.[9]

There is some feeling that the potential benefits of rent regulation in the United Kingdom have been corroded by the complexities and uncertainties of rent assessment boards, rent tribunals, and rent scrutiny boards. Furnished tenants, for example, may hesitate to bring rent cases before rent tribunals because of the possibility that the tribunal may decide to increase rather than reduce their rents, or out of fear that an application for decreased rent will be quickly followed by a notice to quit from the landlord. In the latter case, an appeal can be made for security of tenure, but even if granted, it only remains effective for six months (although extensions are sometimes obtainable).

Despite the benefits tenants derive from rent control in the form of decreased cost of housing, it appears that there are very serious long-term effects of pursuing such a policy. Rent control has contributed to the housing problem in both New York and the United Kingdom through preventing adequate maintenance and discouraging new investment. The Rand Institute concludes that

---

[b]Ira S. Lowry, Joseph S. DeSalvo, and Barbara Woodfell, *Rental Housing in New York City, Vol. II, The Demand for Shelter* (New York: Rand Institute, 1972), p. 86. Of course, two caveats should be kept in mind: (1) uncontrolled housing was newer than controlled housing and thus would be expected to be structurally sounder, and (2) a large portion of market rent and estimated market rent may have been due to location factors, with the controlled units concentrated in high value locations such as Manhattan.

"the city's [New York's] system of rent control has achieved its principal objectives, the protection of tenants from 'unfair' rent increases in a tight housing market. But by preventing rents from rising in step with the cost of supplying rental housing, it has left owners with few alternatives to undermaintenance and reduction of building services."[10]

Size and Scope of the Private Rental Sector

In the United Kingdom, some critics have accused more than half a century of rent control legislation of having effectively destroyed the private rental sector. Indeed, as can be seen in Table 4-1, the private rental sector has been steadily declining. At the end of the First World War, an estimated 90 percent of all dwellings were in this sector. By 1972 only 13 percent of all dwelling units were in the private rental sector (or 18 percent if housing association units are included). The Other Non-Public Rental category shown in the table includes housing association rental housing and cooperatives.

By comparison, the private rental sector in the United States is still relatively large, although there has been a substantial drop since World War II, as shown in Table 4-2. During the last two years there has been a further decline as a combination of nationally imposed rent-control, though a temporary policy, and a shortage of units for sale to owner-occupiers caused by the rapid decline in homebuilding as interest rates rose and money became tight, has contributed to the conversion of an increasing number of existing rental units to condominia. These are individually owned units in a multi-unit building with maintenance of the common areas performed by a management company paid through a

Table 4-1
Stock of Dwellings in Great Britain, by Tenure, 1947-1972

	1947	1950	1960 (United Kingdom only)	1966	1970	1972
1. Private Rental		44.6	25.9	18.9	14.9	13
2. Other Non-Public Rental		7.9	5.6	5.7	5.1	5
Totals 1 & 2	61	52.5	31.5	24.3	20.0	18

Source: David Donnison, *The Government of Housing* (London: Penguin, 1967), p. 186; U.K. Central Statistical Office, *Social Trends*, HMSO, No. 4, 1973, p. 156; Stuart Lansley and Guy Fiegehan, *Housing Allowances & Inequality*, Young Fabian Pamphlet, H36 (London: Fabian Society, 1973), p. 6.

Table 4-2
U.S. Private Rental Units as a Percent of Total Units, 1900-1970

1900	1910	1920	1930	1940	1950	1960	1970
53.3	54.1	54.4	52.2	56.4	45.0	37	35.3

Note: The figures for 1970 include federally subsidized, privately owned rental units, but exclude public housing.
Source: U.S., Department of Commerce, Bureau of the Census, *Statistical Abstract of the United States, 1973*, GPO, 1973, p. 689.

condominium fee assessed on all the owners. For many families, condominia apparently fulfill the financial and psychological advantages of homeownership without imposing the same degree of responsibility as does a traditional free-standing single family unit.

This decline in the privately rented sector in the United States over a thirty-year period can nevertheless hardly have been caused by rent control. It instead is almost certainly due primarily to rising incomes and a strong socio-cultural preference for homeownership.

Certainly the same process is evident in the United Kingdom, although it clearly cannot account for all or perhaps even the greatest portion of the private rental sector's precipitous decline, particularly since movement from the rental sector has occurred equally into public sector rental housing as well as owner-occupation. The other causes can be found in the history of public policy in which pursuit of economic and social objectives that at times were only remotely concerned with the state of the private rental market has made investment in that sector uneconomic except for higher income units.

Within this framework, rent control is surely a contributing factor to the decline of the private rental sector but it is not the only one. The private rental sector has been disadvantaged through taxation and subsidy policy relative to both owner-occupied and public sector housing. In the United Kingdom, tax laws do not permit owners of residential rental property to deduct the cost of depreciation of their capital asset from income subject to taxation. As Della Nevitt comments:

> The tax laws of the United Kingdom have taken no account of the fact that a dwelling unit has only a limited life. Taxes on residential property are imposed on the assumption that dwellings last forever and that sinking funds are a luxury which some landlords like to have and others do not. The annual payments into the fund are not regarded as a necessity and are not, therefore, classified for tax purposes as a cost.[11]

This provision, combined with rent-control legislation limiting the gross return the landlord could receive from rent increases following capital improvement, made it almost impossible for landlords to improve or refurnish their holdings unless the property had a life of thirty or more years after improvement.[12] The result is that the private rental sector now comprises the poorest quality housing in the United Kingdom.

Owner-occupied housing is heavily subsidized through mortgage interest deductions from income liable to taxation (at the same time, the imputed rental income gained by the owner from his occupation of the unit is *not* taxed)[c] and by the exclusion from capital gains taxation of capital gains derived from sale of an owner-occupied home. In the first case, owners of residential rental property may deduct mortgage interest payments as expenses, but they may do so only by offsetting it against gross rental income from the property, whereas owner-occupiers can offset interest deductions against any income. And, of course, the owner of rental property must pay taxes on his net rental income, while the owner-occupier does not. In the second case, rental properties are subject to a tax from which owner-occupiers are exempt.

The private rental sector is similarly disadvantaged relative to public sector housing that receives government subsidies from local rates and from the central government. In addition, public sector housing can reduce costs by pooling revenue and offsetting the cost of new units against the much lower cost of older units, while this option is not available to the fractionated private rental sector where individual holdings are quite small.

By contrast, U.S. tax and subsidy policy—while treating owner-occupiers considerably more favorably than tenants—has not been as discouraging to the rental sector. Not only is depreciation of residential property allowed as a deduction from taxable income, but the depreciation methods used greatly increase the value of this benefit to investors. A new apartment building may be depreciated for tax purposes at an accelerated rate either through the declining balance method or the sum of the year's digits method. In the former case, the investor may depreciate the property at up to 200 percent the rate of straight line depreciation (which is in itself an overstatement of true depreciation), each year subtracting the amount depreciated from the total value of the property. Used apartments can be depreciated at a rate of 125 percent on the declining balance basis. In the latter (sum of the years) method, the property is depreciated according to a ratio that is applied to its full value. The numerator of the ratio is, each year, the number of years remaining in the property's life; the denominator is the same every year—the sum of all the years of the property's full life.

The subsidy derived from these devices is substantial. A study by Paul Taubman and Robert Rasche concluded that using only a straight line depreciation method rather than true depreciation would confer a subsidy of 14 percent of purchase price, while use of the double declining balance method could yield a subsidy of double that.[13] In some cases, the benefits are even greater. Federal

---
[c]It was taxable prior to 1963 (Schedule A).

tax law provides for the entire cost of rehabilitating low-income rental property (assuming it remains such after it has been rehabilitated) to be depreciated over a five-year period.

An effort is made by the federal government to recapture some of the subsidy conferred by accelerated depreciation through taxation at ordinary income tax rates of that portion of any capital gain (sales price minus depreciated value) that is due to the excess of accelerated depreciation over straight line depreciation. Normally, capital gains are taxable at half the rate of ordinary income. However, after 17 years (10 years with respect to the federally subsidized rental program) the entire capital gain is taxable at normal capital gain rates. All these deductions, including deductions for mortgage interest payments and local property tax, are made enormously valuable because, unlike the case in the United Kingdom, they can be deducted from the owner's total income rather than simply from the property's rental income. Obviously an individual must have a good deal of income in order to make use of these tax shelters.

Despite these tax advantages to owners of rental property, it is clear that so far as an occupant is concerned, he is better off owning his home than renting. If he is a homeowner, he is able to deduct both mortgage interest and local property tax from his income liable to taxation (presumably on the assumption that they are expenses incurred in the production of income), yet at the same time the imputed rental income produced is not taxable. As a result of these subsidies, Henry Aaron calculates that two households, each of four people, each with $15,000 annual earned income and housing costs of $3750, alike in all respects except that one household rents its residence and the other owns it, would pay taxes that differed by $600: the renting household would pay $2150 in taxes compared to $1,556 for the owner-occupant.[14]

Condition of the Private Rental Sector

Despite the relatively (compared to the United Kingdom) substantial size of the private rental sector in the United States, it is in this sector that both countries experience their most severe problems.

Given the heavy disadvantages imposed by public policy on private rental housing in the United Kingdom, it is not surprising that the most serious housing problems are located there. The National House Condition Survey conducted in 1971 showed that 54 percent of all housing unfit for human habitation in England and Wales (nearly 1.2 million dwelling units) was located in the private rental sector, although this sector represented about 18 percent of the total stock. Nearly 23 percent of units in the private rental sector were unfit compared to 1 percent of local authority housing and 4 percent of owner-occupied housing.[15] More than 31 percent of all units in the private rental sector had no toilet inside the unit compared to only 5.6 percent of local authority units and 7.8 percent of owner-occupied units.[16] Furthermore, private sector rental housing is extremely old; nearly 70 percent of all such units were built before 1919 compared to 3.7 percent of council house units and 34.1 percent of owner-occupied units.[17] Finally, private sector rental housing is occupied by those at the lowest levels of the income scale: the median income for a household in the private unfurnished sector was £1,325 in 1971 compared to £1,611 for local authority residents, and about £1,980 for owner-occupiers.[18]

Clearly the worst housing is that portion of stock in the privately rented furnished sector. There are about 600,000 such units in the United Kingdom—about 3 percent of total housing stock. Nearly 50 percent of all furnished units are in London.[19] The Francis Committee found that compared to the unfurnished rental sector, furnished accommodation had inferior amenities, greater overcrowding, and higher rent, although the actual physical condition of the dwelling was slightly better.[20]

Given the legal framework within which it must operate in the United Kingdom, private residential rental property cannot generate enough income to provide adequate maintenance or services. It certainly cannot generate enough income to attract any new investment, and it is becoming increasingly difficult to even retain present investment. The recent rapid increases in house prices for owner-occupancy have caused a rush on the part of owners to obtain vacant possession (an easy task in furnished tenancies since security of tenure does not exist), and sell their property for owner-occupancy as a means of recouping—and in most cases substantially enhancing—their original capital investment.

The result has been a severe shortage of private rental property and an increase in the number of homeless people or families who must either double up with other households in overcrowded dwellings or be temporarily housed by the local council in hostels or bed and breakfast accommodations. The problem of homelessness is apparently intensifying and is the most publicized and emotion-laden housing issue in the United Kingdom.[d]

In the United States, a substantial proportion of all housing classified as "dilapidated" was in the rental sector,[e] although this sector represented about 37 percent of all housing. Slightly more than 8 percent of all rental units lacked some or all plumbing facilities compared to 4.5 percent of owner-occupied units. Of the rental units, 52 percent were constructed prior to 1939 compared to 37 percent of owner-occupied units. And a higher proportion of low-income people

---

[d]It also has given rise to a substantial squatting movement, particularly in London, where several groups exist to move families into unoccupied units awaiting demolition or sale, or being held for speculation. Squatting is relatively infrequent in the United States compared to the United Kingdom. Nonetheless, it is not unknown.

[e]These figures from the U.S. *Statistical Abstract*, include all rental housing, including public housing and federally subsidized housing, which in total accounts for about 7 to 8 percent of all rental housing. The figures thus probably slightly overestimate the quality of the private rental housing.

occupied rental units (58 percent) than owned homes (42 percent). These aggregate data, while they obscure the much more serious condition of the rental stock in many low-income central city areas, nevertheless demonstrate on the whole that (1) as in the United Kingdom, the private rental sector in the United States is worse off than the owner-occupied sector, and (2) taken as an aggregate, the private rental system in the United States is not as badly off, relative to the owner-occupied sector, as is its U.K. counterpart.

Part of the explanation for the better condition of the private residential rental sector in the United States, compared to Britain, must be the much greater rent, both in absolute terms and as a percent of income that Americans are willing to pay for housing. In 1971, the median monthly rent in the United States was $95 and the rent-household income ratio was 20.9 percent, while in 1972 in the United Kingdom, the median weekly rent paid in the private rental sector was £2.73 (or about £11.73 per month) and the median rebated rent-household income ratio was less than 11 percent. Partly this represents the restrictive impact of rent control, but to some extent it also reflects historic differences in the amount British citizens are accustomed, and thus expect, to pay for housing. These figures include rates. They thus are roughly comparable to rent statistics in the United States where property taxes are levied on the owner who, as much as possible, passes them on to the tenants in higher rent. However, the traditional low housing cost-income ratio has been shattered during the past few years, particularly in the London area, by explosive increases in home prices and in the rents of uncontrolled rental dwellings. The public response to this, not unnaturally, has been one of shock and resentment and reimposition of stricter rent controls.

As these figures imply, rental property in the United States would seem more capable of generating a rental income sufficient to provide a reasonable return than it does in the United Kingdom. Indeed, compared to the United Kingdom, the private rental market in the United States, in aggregate, is still a flourishing industry attracting substantial new investment. In 1972, 45 percent of all new non-public sector housing starts were multi-family rental units,[21] while in the United Kingdom, less than 5 percent of new starts were in the private rental sector.

The impressive aggregate U.S. figures, however, mask perhaps the most important housing problem the United States faces—the condition of housing in the low-income sector of the private rental market and of the very viability of that sector of the market itself. The part of the private rental market that is "flourishing" is the middle- and upper-middle-income portion, not the low-income part (at least it was flourishing prior to the imposition of rent control during Phase I and to the precipitous decline in housing starts in 1973 and 1974, both of which have been factors in encouraging the conversion of a substantial number of middle income rental units to condominiums). Thus, the median rent of new apartments completed in 1971 was $185 per month—nearly double the median rent of existing units. Only 16 percent of these new units rented for less than $150 per month, and 37 percent rented for more than $200 per month.[22]

The market for low-income people, particularly in inner-city areas, has deteriorated badly. In fact, some of the largest American cities have experienced a near collapse in this sector over the last decade with consequences for tenants similar to those in the United Kingdom. Soaring real estate taxes and operating costs, high turnover rates (meaning units are frequently empty and not continuously generating rents), and losses due to vandalism—all within the context of deteriorating landlord-tenant relations in the wake of the racial turmoil of the 1960s—have nearly destroyed inner-city rental housing as a viable investment. Rents cannot be raised high enough to generate an economic return, not because of rent control as in the United Kingdom, but simply because of the low-income of central city tenants and the resulting inadequate demand (if they were raised sufficiently to provide for adequate maintenance and a reasonable return, rent-income ratios would be intolerably high). The result is invariably inadequate maintenance and a consequent deterioration in the housing stock, and not infrequently actual abandonment of the property by the owner. It is estimated that there are nearly 100,000 such units in New York alone. These are units—many of which when abandoned were physically sound structures—from which the owner simply walked away because he could no longer afford to operate them. Thus, 80 percent of the units abandoned in New York City during 1968 were in buildings classified only three years earlier as sound or deteriorating, but not dilapidated.[23]

The vacant units are rarely withheld from the market for speculative purposes; indeed, in many cases, the owner also cedes control of the property either through tax foreclosure proceedings for non-payment of property taxes or through paper sales at nominal values in order to rid himself of legal liabilities. Unlike London, there is no real market for these properties. There is currently little demand for converting these inner-city properties, mostly in black ghettoes, into owner-occupied homes for the middle class (although there are exceptions such as Georgetown and Capitol Hill in Washington, D.C.—the American equivalent of what in the United Kingdom is called "gentrification").

After his intensive study of the Baltimore inner-city housing market, Stegman concluded:

The inner-city inventory appears to have deteriorated since 1960 and continues to deteriorate today ... that this decline in quality is associated with a collapse of the inner-city market; that a substantial proportion of investor-owners are experiencing negative cash flows, largely because of excessive operating costs rather than low rents; that most investors want to get out of the business; that most of the inventory is no longer as well managed as it once was; and that vandalism and abandonment is taking its toll on good as well as poor housing, and at a faster rate than government programs are adding subsidized units to the stock.[24]

The collapse of the low-income inner-city market has had serious consequences for residents of such neighborhoods. During the 1960s there was a substantial net loss in low-cost housing. According to the Joint Center study:

> After correcting for inflation, we find over the decade of the 1960s a net loss of 2.1 million units renting for less than $100 per month (in 1970 dollars), even though 1.2 million such units were constructed during the same period. In percentage terms this represents a loss of 16 percent of the low-rent stock ... Thus, because of losses through demolition and rent increases due to renovation, and because of economic pressures on landlords, the stock of low-rent units is diminishing.[25]

Demand for low-cost units may well have decreased during the 1960s as well because of rising real incomes, but surely not as sharply as supply. Thus the Joint Center concludes that there has been a dramatic shift in the pattern of housing deprivation from occupancy in physically inadequate units to occupancy of physically adequate units but with high-rent burden (defined as a two-or-more-person household paying more than 25 percent of its income for rent or a single-person household paying more than 35 percent of its income for rent). The number of households living in physically adequate housing but with a high-rent burden increased from 3.67 million in 1960 (comprising 24 percent of all households with housing deprivation) to 5.5 million households in 1970 (42 percent of all households with housing deprivation).[f]

Remedies

The deteriorating state of the private rental sector is thus a most vexing problem for current housing policy in both countries. What solutions have been attempted or proposed?

In the United Kingdom, there appears to be general agreement—with some dissent—that a revival of that sector is quite unlikely and, in the minds of some, quite undesirable anyway for ideological reasons. Changes in government policy are unlikely to reverse the decline unless those changes persist through several different governments. The problem is lack of investor confidence and that is unlikely to be revived so long as the view persists that any remedial changes

---

[f]David Birch et al., *America's Housing Needs: 1970 to 1980* (Cambridge, Mass.: Joint Center for Urban Studies, 1973), p. 4-10. The study identified three components of housing deprivation: (1) physically inadequate housing, (2) overcrowding, and (3) high-rent burden. In 1970, 13.1 million households suffered from one or more forms of housing deprivation: 52 percent of these lived in physically inadequate housing, 5 percent in physically adequate but overcrowded housing (another 5 percent lived in physically inadequate *and* overcrowded), and 42 percent in non-overcrowded, physically adequate housing but with a high-rent burden (an additional 11 percent lived in physically inadequate and/or overcrowded housing with a high-rent burden).

enacted by a Conservative government will simply be repealed by a future Labour government. Imposition of a new rent freeze by the new Labour Government in March, 1974 to set aside rent regulation vividly illustrates the essential accuracy of this view.

Sensitivity to the problems and conditions of private rental sector tenants is a rather recent development in British policy. Despite their statutory commitment to assess total housing needs within their jurisdiction, many local housing authorities apparently pursue a rather limited view of their responsibilities. They define their purview as limited to the building, allocating, and management of council housing. The Seebohm Committee criticized this "waiting list" philosophy and recommended that "all housing authorities should, we consider, take a comprehensive and extended view of their responsibilities to meet the housing needs of their area. In particular, they should be generally concerned with assisting a family to obtain and keep adequate accommodation whether *it be in the council house sector or not* [italics added]."[26]

The Institute of Housing Managers, the professional organization of local housing officials, has warmly embraced this social service-oriented concept as an ideology. Its crux is that local housing authorities will be responsible for improving the housing conditions of all those residing in the local authority rather than solely those residing in publicly owned housing within that authority.

At present, a strong body of opinion within the Labour Party favors a policy of "municipalization" or social ownership of the great bulk of the private rental stock as the only means by which the conditions of tenants in the private sector could be improved. Presumably this would be accompanied by compensation at market value to private owners (except for unfit units, which would be acquired at site value only[g]) and a substantial investment of public funds to rehabilitate, improve, and maintain these units. Using data from the 1971 House Condition Survey of England and Wales, we can estimate that the total cost of repair local authorities would have to undertake if they acquired dwellings in the private rental sector and put them into condition to let for 20 years would be in excess of £1 billion.[27] And this does not include the cost of installing basic amenities if they do not now exist.

The local authority would then have the capability of manipulating the totality of rental housing resources within its jurisdiction on behalf of its citizens. It could pursue a fully "rational" housing policy by matching household need with the characteristics of the available rental stock. Despite the attractions of this kind of comprehensive municipalization, the vision of all

---
[g]At present local authorities already have the power to issue compulsory purchase orders to acquire private property for housing uses, subject, however, to the approval of the Department of Environment. Compensation is paid at market value assuming no change in planning (i.e., existing use value) except for unfit buildings, which are compensated at site value only.

rental housing in a jurisdiction under the administration of a rather monolithic and unresponsive bureaucracy with a central allocation system and, at least presently, severe constraints on mobility ought to give some pause. In his Fabian Tract, "Rented Housing and Social Ownership," Malcolm Wicks considers this problem and attempts to deal with it by building in diversity within publicly responsible sector:

Simple municipalization would mean one public body controlling all rented accommodation in an area. This would be extremely undesirable. At worst it could lead to grave abuse and the victimisation of individuals who had displeased the local council. It would also give less incentive to innovations in housing management which could well occur given healthy rivalry between different public bodies fulfilling the same role. The absence of a monopoly would better ensure that minority social groups were given their proper consideration. Social ownership in practice therefore should mean a variety of publicly responsible bodies providing housing. . . . The acquiring authorities (local authorities) should not, however, keep all accommodation in the long term. They should seek to hand over a fair proportion to housing associations and co-operatives as soon as possible.[28]

Similarly, the Society of Labour Lawyers writes:

Although the case for the municipalization of privately rented property is in our view firmly established, there has been surprisingly little discussion of the detailed steps required to put it into effect. It will take great forethought to ensure that the measures taken result in more people living in better conditions without freezing everyone into their existing accommodation. Unless adequate precautions are taken, municipalization could result in a situation in which it became virtually impossible for a tenant to move to another area to break up an unhappy marriage or for children to set up home away from in-laws without waiting to come to the top of a local authority housing list.[29]

Whatever one's view of the merits of comprehensive municipalization, it does seem relevant to ask how the case for it can be so "firmly established" when its most enthusiastic proponents admit that no one has thought through how to assure that the actual housing conditions people experience will not deteriorate as a consequence.

The assignment of houses by local authorities at present is based on waiting lists and point systems that greatly impede mobility. The process is fraught, on the whole, and perhaps unavoidably, with bureaucratic rule fixation and inflexibility that often results in an insensitivity to human needs. Furthermore, housing authorities have shown a great propensity to favor families with children at the expense of students, single individuals, both young and old, the elderly, and those who for one reason or another are mobile or transient. The privately rented sector now houses a disproportionate share of these groups. How will they fare under municipalization? It is not, of course, necessary to retain rental accommodation in the hands of traditional private investors in order to avoid these possible pitfalls of municipalization. There is nothing inherent in the nature of private ownership that makes it impossible for any other form to satisfy these needs.

The Society of Labour Lawyers does, in fact, go on to observe that the private rental sector has provided a "safety valve" in the past and that "until local authorities and housing associations are able to provide accommodation immediately upon request (a situation unlikely to be reached in the stress areas until a good many years after the social ownership programme is completed) some such safety valve will certainly be needed."[30] The safety valve the Society suggests is new tax incentives to encourage owner-occupiers and local authority tenants to rent out rooms. Since the shortage problem will probably worsen as a result of municipalization (assuming local authorities will not accept the kind of overcrowding that exists at present in the private rental sector and assuming tenants in the worst private rental units must be housed elsewhere when their present units are rehabilitated or even demolished), it seems doubtful that the letting or subletting of rooms will prove nearly adequate.

If "social ownership" of some sort is desirable (and it may well be within the British context), then its justification must be that it will result in better housing for people. It is difficult to avoid the conclusion that the rationale for comprehensive municipalization so far is based more on the obvious problems of the privately rented sector under present arrangements and ideological purity rather than any real analysis of what peoples' housing conditions will be as a result.

The Labour Government has in fact approached municipalization in a much more tentative and piecemeal way than the advocates of comprehensive municipalization have urged. Building on preliminary initiatives by the previous Conservative Government, it issued a circular in April 1974 that provided guidance to local authorities for municipalization activities. The circular stated:

The Secretaries of State consider that local authorities, in acquiring property according to their assessment of local needs and in drawing up their initial programmes for acquisition, should concentrate their acquisitions within areas of more acute housing stress. In order to deploy resources towards tackling bad housing conditions most effectively, local authorities should therefore identify those areas in which housing and social action is most urgent, and firmly relate their acquisition of existing dwellings to them.[31]

The circular then sets out five circumstances under which local authorities may proceed with municipalization. It is unclear from this list to what extent the local authority is encouraged to proceed by buying property for sale on the open market and to what extent it is expected to proceed by issuing compulsory purchase orders, which must be approved by the central government. The five circumstances listed are:

a. acquisition made in pursuance of a confirmed compulsory purchase order or to meet a statutory obligation to acquire a particular property;
b. acquisition, particularly in areas of acute housing stress, of tenanted property where the local authority has clear evidence that tenants are in need as a result of bad housing conditions, including threat of harassment and risk of becoming homeless;
c. acquisition of properties which have been standing empty for six months, or of properties with vacant possession in which there is a severe overall shortage of housing *and* the acquisition of which would be for the purposes of housing essential public service employees or the homeless;
d. houses previously sold by a local authority which they are re-acquiring under the terms of a pre-emption clause imposed on the original sale;
e. acquisition on behalf of, or in order to sponsor, a housing association or a tenants' co-operative.[32]

The government then made available £141 million in loan authority to the Greater London Council for its municipalization program during the 1974-75 year and £56 million to local authorities outside London. So long as the municipalization fell within one of the five categories, local authorities did not have to request permission from the central government to use the loan authority for specific cases. However, as all compulsory purchase orders of any kind must be approved by the central government, the government retains its ability to modulate the pace of municipalization.

In the United States, the problems of the low-income private rental sector have called forth some social service-oriented responses to improve the housing conditions of inner-city residents. So far, none have been particularly successful, and the result of many of them has been a sort of municipalization by default. Unfortunately, fiscally hard-pressed American cities are in no better position to absorb the operating loss than are private landlords, and therefore the repairs and maintenance necessary to assure adequate housing services to tenants have seldom been forthcoming even under public ownership. Sternlieb discusses the public response:

Foreclosure Proceedings
There is a very considerable range of tax foreclosure proceedings utilised by U.S. municipalities. These range from one to four or more years before foreclosure proceedings can be instituted. Not uncommonly, the latter in turn may involve as much as a year of court proceedings before clear title can be secured. In the interim the parcels are obviously run down very severely, and not uncommonly end up beyond recall. . . . The basic concept of low-income housing market is one in which the incomes derived from properties are adequate both to service those properties and to keep the owners in business. This has in turn engendered a variety of punitive measures to insure maintenance. Unfortunately, in many cases these have backfired.

The impacts of code enforcement without a realistic view of the market has been touched on before. It may be appropriate here, however, to indicate some of the experiences in Chicago along this line. According to Judge Kral of

Chicago's Housing Court, as part of the Model Cities, a program of concentrated code enforcement was instituted. This involved the owner being presented with a choice of either fixing up the parcel in question or having it demolished. The economics of the situation are illustrated by the fact that as many as 4000 units in a single year were demolished under the program before it was halted.

Emergency Repair Program
New York City has pioneered a program of having the city provide emergency repairs. If a tenant reports a health-impairing violation, the city makes efforts to make the landlord remedy the situation. If suitable action is not forthcoming from this source, the city undertakes the responsibility for the repairs and in turn presents the landlord with a lien against the structure. The logic and need of such a program is undeniable. The results, however, in a great many cases have been the landlord walking away from the parcel in question and its subsequent demise.

Rent Escrow Programs
Rent escrow programs have been instituted in a number of cities for parcels which do not meet code standard. In this program, rents are collected from the tenants, and held by the municipality or a subsidiary authority. The rents in turn serve as the basis for rehabilitation financing. The concept is that when the structure again meets standard, its rents revert to the owner. Unfortunately, again the flow of funds typically are not found adequate to service the costs of required repairs. The results frequently have been the abandonment of the structure by the private owner and the inheritance by the city of yet another parcel.

The City as the Owner of Last Resort
As the result of these punitive acts against the private market, cities are inheriting increasing numbers of parcels. Unfortunately, there is little in the way of a track record to indicate that municipalities are very much better operators than private owners. The costs of maintenance in the structures which have been examined under this program, particularly in New York, are very high, the delivery of housing services are far from adequate. A new administrative apparatus obviously is going to be required.[33]

It is clear that a substantial public subsidy, whether through municipalization or some other means, will be required. Systematic and explicit municipalization is unlikely in the United States given its political ideology and traditions, although de facto municipalization is already occurring by default with increasing frequency. It has not yet, however, been accompanied by federal subsidies. Direct subsidies to private slum landlords would prove no more palatable in the United States than in the United Kingdom, and while increased tax incentives for investors in rental property are possible, they too would meet with political resistance. In any case, tax incentives would likely be effective only if inner-city property were first transferred to owners who have sufficient income to make use of tax shelters since present owners, on the whole, do not.

Two other possibilities are an indirect subsidy to landlords, such as a housing allowance given to tenants that would thus increase their effective demand (presumably part of this subsidy would also accrue to tenants in the form of better housing conditions), or a subsidy as exists in the present Section 23 program whereby the municipal government rents privately owned dwellings and uses a federal government subsidy to pay the owner an economic return on his investment while letting the unit to a tenant at below market rents. The last two alternatives are being actively considered at the present time, and are discussed elsewhere in this work.[h]

Summary

The problems confronting inner-city rental housing in the United States are not altogether dissimilar to those afflicting the United Kingdom, although the causes may differ somewhat. In both cases, rental income in the private sector is not sufficient to provide adequate housing services and a reasonable return on investment. In the United Kingdom, the result has been a rapid decline in the number of dwellings in the private rental sector. In the United States, the result has been higher rents and a decline in numbers, though less rapid than in the United Kingdom. Proposed remedies have not yet met the problem and in some cases may even have intensified it.

---

[h]In fact, the Housing and Community Development Act of 1974, signed by President Ford in August, both increased funding for an existing experiment to test the feasibility of a housing allowance, and instituted a new Housing Assistance Program similar to the existing Section 23 program. The latter program was provided with more than $800 million in contract authority for fiscal year 1975 and is expected to gradually replace the more traditional public housing approach.

5
Security of Tenure

In both the United States and the United Kingdom, landlord-tenant law is based on the law of property transactions derived from the English Common Law. Property law developed primarily to regulate the transfer of land rather than buildings on land. Its emphasis is on possession: the landlord gives over possession of (leases) the land for a period of time to the tenant who is legally entitled to enjoy possession of the land during that time. The landlord takes no responsibility for the quality of the land or for its upkeep; in fact, he is largely enjoined from interfering with it during the tenant's legal possession so long as the tenant pays the rent. Rent is the quid pro quo of possession. If the tenant fails to pay the rent, he legally loses possession. Likewise, when the lease expires and is not renewed, possession of the land reverts to the landlord.

When this system is applied to the renting of dwelling units (usually in multi-unit buildings) rather than land, the social strains are obvious. As long as the landlord allows the tenant to maintain possession, rent must be paid. Poor maintenance, inadequate service, violation of housing codes, and so forth are not justification for non-payment of rent. The duty to pay rent is independent of any actions of the landlord not threatening possession; it is not conditioned upon adequate performance of a set of responsibilities by the landlord as it would be if governed by the law of contracts rather than property law. Furthermore, the tenant's occupation of the dwelling unit is legal only for the period of the lease (if there is a lease). Beyond that, his home is at the mercy of his landlord's discretion.

This legal imbalance clearly favoring landlord over tenant should be fertile territory for a social service housing policy. British policy has indeed reacted by providing security-of-tenure legislation (in effect mandating a return to an earlier era of de facto long leases but staying largely within the bounds of property law[a]), while American policy has reacted more slowly, ignoring the security-of-tenure problem but employing the judicial process to evolve a landlord-tenant law increasingly based on the law of contracts rather than property law. This evolution is still in process and has a long way to go, but its outlines can at least now be seen.

Security-of-tenure legislation in the United Kingdom is a logical partner of rent control. Obviously provisions guaranteeing security of tenure are useless without some form of rent regulation because landlords could otherwise

---
[a]Furnished units *are* assumed to have an implied warrant of habitability at the commencement of tenancy.

effectively evict tenants by simply increasing their rents. Likewise a system of rent control involving decontrol after change of possession requires security of tenure else landlords achieve decontrol simply by evicting their tenant. Any system of rent control resting upon tenant appeal for enforcement likewise requires security-of-tenure legislation; otherwise tenants will decline to go to the authorities for fear of eviction. In fact, without security of tenure, landlords will be strongly tempted to charge illegal rents above controlled levels and to threaten eviction if reported. Finally, security of tenure may be required if rent control is in effect in order to forestall landlord efforts to capitalize the market rent they are forbidden by selling the unit for owner-occupation, thereby depriving the tenant of the benefits of rent control.

Della Nevitt, in fact, argues that the primary benefit of rent control is not lower accommodation prices but the security of tenure and the well-specified legal rights and responsibilities that must accompany it. She writes: "Universal measures of rent control are merely a substitute for individually drawn contracts. The system would always be redundant if all tenants consulted a solicitor before entering into a tenancy agreement and obtaining a properly drawn lease . . . rent control may be regarded simply but accurately as the poor and/or uneducated man's lease."[1]

Thus, when rent-control legislation was enacted in the United Kingdom in 1915, security-of-tenure provisions logically followed. However, security of tenure can also be seen as a fundamental value in itself rather than simply a necessary accompaniment to rent control. Social policy can pursue the objective of security and certainty of a family's homeplace as a human need that government should assure for renters as well as owner-occupiers. The Labour Party tends to view security of tenure more in the light of a fundamental value, while the Conservatives see it more as a logical necessity if rent control is to exist.

At the present time, virtually all occupants of the private, unfurnished rental sector in the United Kingdom are given security of tenure. They cannot be dispossessed from their home except for non-payment of rent or conduct that is a nuisance to other occupants and even then only after application to a county court and only if the court deems the removal "reasonable." Prior to 1965, landlords could simply evict tenants who did not have security of tenure by giving four weeks notice to quit. Now all evictions also require a court order, including evictions of tenants who do not have security.

The effect of security of tenure is that all covered tenants have lifetime leases; indeed the statutory tenancy can be passed on twice after the original tenant's death to other members of the family. Sale of the dwelling unit to another owner does not negate the statutory tenancy, nor does the intention of converting the building for other uses. The court may grant a landlord a possession order if he can show that suitable alternative accommodation is available for the tenant, but in areas of housing shortage such as London, this is difficult to prove. Thus, landlords who wish to convert the building to another use, or sell for such conversion, must either "bribe" the tenant to move with a cash payment, or wait until one by one all his tenants have moved (assuming he cannot find them suitable alternative accommodations). The 1965 Rent Act also provided a penalty of £100 or imprisonment for up to six months for harassment of tenants, which thus diminishes (but not eliminates) the possible use of this effective mechanism for removing a sitting tenant.[b]

If a landlord wishes to sell the building, he will be quite loath to do so until all tenants have left, since the selling price will be much higher "with vacant possession" (no tenants) than with tenants remaining. As a result, security-of-tenure legislation, although it has accomplished its primary goal of protecting the sitting tenant, has also had the unintended consequence of encouraging landlords wishing to sell or convert to keep flats empty even in the face of a severe housing shortage. It has also greatly discouraged new investment in private rental housing since the owner of such housing has, in effect, invested in an asset that is *very* immobile and illiquid—much more so than most other investments, including most other property investments.

Until the summer of 1974, furnished tenants did not have security of tenure, which situation was strongly criticized by activist housing groups but which the Labour Government changed shortly after assuming office. Thus a Shelter (National Campaign for the Homeless) pamphlet argued:

The insecurity of furnished tenants is unquestionably the key problem in areas of housing stress, particularly in London. Although furnished tenants are most often those who must share household facilities and who suffer in a poor housing situation, the ease with which they can be evicted has proved to be the most significant issue in such areas.[2]

Prior to the change, furnished tenants could apply to Rent Tribunals to receive security of tenure for six-month periods (with possible extensions), but the main purpose of this respite was to provide time for tenants to search for new dwellings rather than to guarantee occupation in their present dwellings. Opposition to granting security of tenure to furnished tenants was and is based on the fear that it will accelerate the drying up of housing in the private market and only exacerbate problems in the long run. Interestingly, residents of local authority housing also do not have legal security of tenure, although it is generally agreed that local housing authorities act responsibly and sensitively in this regard, and the lack of legal right is not a source of difficulty.

In the United States, tenants are usually on short-term leases (yearly or

---

[b]During the first five years (until March 1970) only 684 prosecutions were brought under this act and only 359 of these resulted in conviction. (U.K., *Report of the Committee on the Rent Acts*, Cmnd. 4609, 1971, p. 104.) The average fine was less than £20 (ibid.). Probably the greatest impact of the act has been upon public attitudes concerning what is acceptable landlord behavior, attitudes which in turn may impose some constraints upon landlords.

monthly) or on no leases at all. Most low-income tenants of inner-city areas are probably, for all practical purposes, tenants at will. A recent survey of low-income households in Baltimore disclosed that only 11 percent recalled signing leases for their present dwelling units.[c] Landlords can regain possession after the lease, if there is one, expires by serving a notice to quit and, if the tenant does not quit on the appointed day, obtaining a summary eviction order from the local court. The tenant basically has no defense during this procedure. However, several states have recently passed legislation—or have had court rulings—prohibiting retaliatory evictions (i.e., evictions that are held to result in retaliation for the tenant's exercise of his legal rights, such as reporting code violations or participating in rent strikes where they are legal). Obviously this prohibition of retaliatory evictions is a rather slender reed for a tenant to rest his hopes on since it depends upon a finding of the landlord's intent and, even when given, provides security for only a limited period of time, usually up to six months.

However, most involuntary moves due to insecurity of tenure never reach the court system, nor would suits to prevent them be successful under present legal arrangements if they did. In his study of low-income households in Baltimore, Rosenberg found that about one-quarter of them had moved within a three-year period and that nearly 20 percent of the households who had moved felt that the move had been involuntary. Of this group of 4,030 involuntary movers, one-third (1,340) were displaced as a result of private market action: 460 of these attributed their displacement to trouble with the landlord; 790 to an increase in rent; and 90 to the sale of the units in which they were living. The other two-thirds (2,690) were displaced as a result of public activity, nearly half (1,210) as a result of the demolition or rehabilitation of their previous dwelling. Another 550 were forced to vacate because of highway construction or urban renewal activity; 200 because they exceeded public housing income limits, and 150 because of code enforcement.[3]

The lack of security of tenure has, probably surprisingly from an Englishman's point of view, not been an important public issue or rallying cry of tenant groups in the United States.[d] Possibly this is due to the relative (compared to the United Kingdom) high vacancy rate in housing markets in the United States

---

[c]Louis Rosenburg, "New Perspectives on Housing Need: A Case Study of the Low-Income Housing Problem in Baltimore, Maryland," unpublished Ph.D. dissertation, Department of City and Regional Planning, University of Pennsylvania, 1973, p. 282. A substantially larger portion may have signed leases but were unable to recall doing so.

[d]The recent rash of conversion of rental units to condominia, however, has brought this issue to the level of public visibility for the first time. existing tenants, although usually given first choice at buying the units in which they are residing, are often not able to do so because the sales price is beyond their reach. Thus many long-standing tenants are evicted and thrown into a housing market where it is increasingly difficult to find rental housing equivalent in quality and cost to that in which they have been residing. Several bills have been introduced in Congress in response to this situation, a certain sign that a problem is in the process of becoming a visible political issue.

and the greater mobility of U.S. population. However, tenant groups *have* been very active, and with some success, in bringing about basic changes in the law governing landlord-tenant relationships, as a recent opinion in the Massachusetts State Supreme Court demonstrates:

The opinion in the Javins Case reflects the view expressed in recent cases and law review articles which rejects the old common law conception of the lease as a property transaction. The modern view favors a new approach which recognises that a lease is essentially a contract between the landlord and the tenant wherein the landlord promises to deliver and maintain the demised premises in habitable condition and the tenant promises to pay rent for such habitable premises.[4]

State legislatures as well as courts have begun to respond by passing laws specifying that residential leases contain implied "Warrants of Habitability." A recent article in the Vanderbilt Law Review summarizes this trend:

The common law traditionally recognized no implied warranty of habitability, warranty of fitness for intended use, or warranty to repair on the part of the landlord in a lease of real property. Because the leasehold was considered an interest in the realty for a term during which the tenant assumed all benefits, obligations and liabilities of ownership, the doctrine of caveat emptor applied, and the tenant accepted the property as he found it at the inception of the lease. Moreover the tenant's obligation for rent was dependent solely on his possessory interest in the real estate. Some jurisdictions have begun more and more to see leases as contracts and have applied doctrine of implied warranty of habitability.

In a number of jurisdictions, statutes create a warranty of habitability on all residential leases or otherwise place upon the landlord the obligation to put and maintain the premises in a habitable condition. Most of these statutes alter the tenant's obligations with respect to paying rent in the event that the landlord breaches his obligation. The statutes are generally of three types:

Rent Abatement: the tenant is relieved of all obligation to pay rent during the duration.

Rent Withholding: the tenant may deposit the rent in judicial escrow until the landlord remedies the breach.

Repair and Deduct: the tenant may make repairs resulting from the landlord's breach and deduct the cost from the rent.[5]

Some states also have laws permitting rent strikes upon the vote of the households residing in the building. As of May 1973, 24 states had legislation or judicial decisions creating, in one form or another, a warrant of habitability for residential rental property.[6] Despite the rapid advance of this trend, one does wonder how much it can realistically achieve without accompanying changes in the legal structure of tenure rights, perhaps through expansion of prohibitions against retaliatory eviction into more positive and lengthy guarantees of security of tenure.

More importantly, one must ask whether the campaign to right the present legal imbalance greatly favoring landlords can, by itself, effect the improvement in slum housing conditions that its proponents foresee. Many who are pursuing this legal reform view the present legal structure as the primary *cause* of slum housing. Thus Quinn and Phillips, writing in the Fordham Law Review, observe:

With the law of landlord-tenant so radically out of balance in favor of the landlord, the consequence was predictable. In ghetto areas, deteriorating structures, rat infestation, and health and the hazards are widespread.[7]

This "slumlord" theory of poor housing has been dismissed as simplistic by economists who have done careful studies of urban housing conditions. Michael Stegman writes:

The notion that owners of low-rent inner-city properties earn exorbitant profits persists in the face of a growing body of contrary evidence. If these profits could only be taxed out of the slums and returned to the occupants in the form of more housing services, it is argued, substandard housing could be significantly improved. Declining inner-city property values, a dearth of potential buyers, and difficulties in maintaining the solvency of subsidized low-rent public housing should constitute sufficient evidence to destroy this myth.[8]

Sternlieb is even more emphatic:

One of the most satisfying figments of folklore in our times is the portrait of the slum landlord. A typical vision is that of the central city slums being the fiefdom of a small group of large investors. The latter in turn grow very fat indeed on the high rents and low input which their tenants and buildings are subjected to.

I have called it a satisfying illusion because it has in turn permitted us the belief that all that is required in low-income housing was a repartitioning of an already adequate rent pie. Whether through code enforcement, rent controls, or any of a host of other mechanisms, the problem of good maintenance could be resolved by squeezing some of the excess profits out of landlords' hands. This process would still leave enough of a residue to maintain his self-interests in the longevity and satisfactory quality of the structure in question.

This bit of folklore may have had considerable validity a decade or two ago. It has little relationship to the realities currently.[9]

Changes in the legal structure, while obviously desirable, may actually worsen housing conditions, unless these changes are accompanied by equivalent changes in the economic viability of low-income inner-city housing (see Chapter 4). The most obvious need is for some form of operating subsidy combined with a change of ownership from small-scale, hard-pressed individual owners, to either (or both) larger-scale professional owners with management expertise or some form of municipal ownership or control.

6

Rent Subsidies and Allowances

Low housing costs as a social service objective may be achieved either through rent control (Chapter 4) or through low rents as a result of public sector subsidization of the capital cost and/or operating costs of buildings (Chapter 3). A third alternate means to this social service goal is through direct rent subsidies to individuals to help them offset the cost of the stated rent. The United Kingdom—and the United States to a much lesser extent—now utilizes this approach in combination with the other two approaches.

Until the Housing Finance Act of 1972, council housing rents were kept low primarily through public subsidies to local housing authorities. Because in some places the resulting rents were still too high for families with limited incomes, local authorities were permitted to run a rent-rebate scheme if they chose to. By 1972, more than half of all authorities did operate such schemes for council tenants.

Public housing rents in the United States are kept low through the same mechanism of public sector subsidy of local housing authorities. In addition, there is a de facto rent rebate for some tenants, since in most cases the rent for a public housing unit is based on a percentage of the tenant's income, subject to a flat minimum and maximum amount. It is thus based primarily on the circumstances of the tenant rather than the dwelling unit. The setting of rents—and thus the exact percentage of income and value of the minimum and maximum—is completely within the jurisdiction of the local housing authority. However, federal law does prohibit any tenant from paying more than 25 percent of adjusted income for rent,[a] even if this amount is less than the set minimum. Thus, some public housing tenants receive, in effect, a rebate equal to the difference between the amount of rent they would have to pay to cover operating costs and the amount they actually pay based on the set percentage of their income or the minimum. Since operating costs must be largely covered out of rent, this means that the rebate is, in effect, paid for out of the higher rents of the relatively more wealthy tenants.

Low housing costs for private sector tenants in the United Kingdom were, until 1972, subsidized by landlords through rent control and regulation. When rent regulation through fair rents was introduced in 1965, the major concern of the Labour Party proponents was not to reduce the burden of the subsidy on the landlord, but to protect tenants from the deregulation effects of the 1957

---

[a]"Adjusted" income is household income minus certain items deducted as expenses (e.g., child care, medical expenses, work-related expenses) and a set exemption per child.

Housing Act and its aftermath. However, "fair rents" nonetheless did result in higher rents for tenants in the great majority of cases so that, in effect, their subsidy through rent control was reduced.

In the United States, rents for private sector tenants are not subsidized at all except for those tenants who reside in federally assisted housing (less than 1 percent of total housing stock). Housing costs for these tenants are subsidized through a combination of all three methods: a public subsidy covering a portion of the capital cost of the building, a basic (controlled) rent, and a rent subsidy equal to the difference between fair-market rent (including a 6 percent return on the equity investment for a limited dividend sponsor) and 25 percent of the tenant's income, subject to the proviso that the tenant must pay at *least* the basic rent and in no case more than the fair-market rent. The basic monthly rent is equal to operating costs plus the capital cost amortized at 1 percent annual interest. An additional "rent supplement" can be used as a "piggyback" to this rental assistance if the basic rent is still more than 25 percent of income. This limited program requires tenants to pay only 25 percent of their income so long as this amounts to at least 30 percent of economic cost.

The Housing Finance Act of 1972 greatly changed the United Kingdom's subsidy system. Subsidization of housing costs through public subsidies in the public sector and rent control in the private sector were greatly reduced since in both sectors, rent levels were henceforth to be set by reference to "fair-rent" criteria. This inevitably meant rent increases for most tenants in both sectors. As a substitute for these subsidies, all local authorities were required to adopt rent-rebate schemes for council house residents and rent-allowance schemes for private rental sector residents.

These rent-subsidy schemes are similar in structure, with one important exception, to those utilized in the U.S. federally assisted rental programs. Tenants must pay a minimum of 40 percent of their rent or £1 per week, whichever is higher. However, if a tenant's "needs allowance" exceeds his income, his minimum rent payment is reduced by 25 percent of the difference between the needs allowance and income; if his needs allowance is less than his income, his minimum rent is increased by 17 percent of the difference up to the fair-rent level as a maximum. The rent subsidy makes up the difference between the tenant's minimum rent payment and the fair rent. The needs allowance is quite substantial, amounting for a family of four to about 60 percent of median income in the United Kingdom. The U.S. system, unlike the British one, sets up an inflexible floor for minimum rent; tenants must pay the basic rent—no matter how low their income—or 25 percent of adjusted income, whichever is higher.

Criticism of the U.K. scheme as a social service device has focused on what the British refer to as the "take-up" problem. Although all local authority tenants and privately rented, unfurnished tenants and some privately rented, furnished tenants are eligible for the rent subsidies, payments are made only upon application. For reasons of lack of information, difficulty in filling out the application form (it is incredibly complex), and stigma, it is feared that considerably less than all those who, in fact, qualify for a rent rebate or allowance will actually apply. The problem is thought to be particularly acute in the private rental sector since it is much easier to convey information and assistance to council house tenants whose names and addresses are known to the local housing authority. Many tenants who, although eligible for a rent allowance, do not actually receive it, will experience substantially increased housing costs if their rents rise due to the new "fair-rent" criteria. Preliminary government figures indicate that nationally 85 percent of eligible council tenants and 50 percent of eligible private tenants are actually receiving the rebate or allowance.[b]

The "take-up" problem is not a problem in the present limited American rent-subsidy scheme because the subsidy is essentially tied to the unit. Tenants residing in the unit pay a rent to the landlord equal to their subsidized (rebated) rent (either basic rent or 25 percent of their income). The difference between the subsidized rent paid by the tenant and cost (fair-market) rent is paid directly to the landlord by the federal government.[c] However, because the subsidy is tied to specific units and because insufficient resources have been made available for the subsidy, many more families are eligible for the subsidy than units exist (this is, of course, similar, although on a much grander scale, to the situation with council housing prior to the Housing Finance Act of 1972). Thus, HUD's estimates indicate that about 20 million households are eligible for its rental assistance program subsidies (there is an income limit for eligibility equal to 135 percent of the limit for public housing eligibility in an area—see Chapter 3), while less than 1 percent actually receive it. The Housing Finance Act avoids this severe equity problem, at least in principle, by making *all* tenants of council housing and private rental unfurnished housing eligible on the same basis.

The second criticism of the U.K. rent subsidies concerns the high marginal tax rate it, in combination with other means-tested benefits and income tax, places on the recipient. In the U.K. system, if a tenant's income exceeds his needs allowance, he loses 17p of his rent subsidy for each additional pound earned; if

---

[b]Peter Wilmott, "Housing" in Michael Young (ed.) *Poverty Report* (London: Temple Smith, 1974), p. 148. Wilmott points out that a survey in Bethnal Green indicated 60 percent of eligible council tenants there were receiving the subsidy compared to only 23 percent of those eligible in the private sector.

[c]It is fair to observe that the take-up problem is a very real one for other American programs, particularly welfare and social service ones, where many who are eligible for benefits for one reason or another do not apply even though they are entitled to receive them. However, there is not as much concern about low take-up rates in the United States as in the United Kingdom, a fact which can probably be explained with reference to the greater emphasis Americans place on individual responsibility and choice (there is probably also a presumption that potential recipients have information that in fact they do not have). The attitude is basically, "You can lead a horse to water, but you can't make him drink." The gap between participants and eligibles also results in keeping program costs down. Although few would publicly argue for this as a method for achieving economy, nonetheless many do regard the effect, whatever its cause, as salutary.

income is less than the needs allowance, he loses 25p of his rent subsidy for each additional pound earned. If the tenant is also paying income tax (which, for a family of four, would commence at a salary of £1,115 per year), he would be paying an additional 30 percent (the basic tax rate for up to £5,000 of taxable earned income) of each pound earned. And there may be other means-tested benefits or income-related contributions (such as social security for which 5 percent of income between £9 and £54 must be paid). The result is a "poverty trap"—an income range within which substantial increases in earned income may result in relatively small increase in disposable income because of the cumulative effect of all the taxes and loss of benefits imposed.

The same problem exists in the U.S. subsidy system where the effective marginal tax rate of an extra dollar earned is 25 percent for residents of Section 236 rental assistance units and averages 20 percent for public housing residents. Income tax does not cause as much of a problem since a family of four pays nothing until its income reaches $4,300, and its tax rate for the first $500 of taxable income amounts to only 14 percent. (American income tax, unlike the British equivalent, is graduated sharply at the lower levels. It is also lower throughout the entire income scale.) However, the poverty-trap problem is greatly exacerbated (in fact it is largely caused) by the welfare system. Welfare recipients are allowed to retain $30 per month plus one-third of anything over that amount of any earnings. This amounts to a marginal tax rate of 66-2/3 percent on earned income of over $30 per month. Food stamps is another means-tested benefit. Anyone who receives all these benefits may have a very substantial marginal tax rate, even though some of the taxes are applied on the net income remaining after others are first applied.

The exact impact of increased income on housing costs for welfare recipients living in federally assisted housing will depend on the system for calculating housing needs as part of public assistance grants. For those states that count actual housing costs as part of a recipient's need for public assistance, there will be no adverse effect. Their increased income will call forth increased housing costs, which, in turn, will simply be paid for by public assistance.[d] For those states that provide a flat public assistance grant, a part of which includes the average value for housing costs in the state, the result will be higher housing costs as each dollar of extra income left over after the public assistance tax rate is applied will require extra housing costs of $.25 (or the relevant figure in public housing).

Much of the criticism of the British rent allowances and rebates has been directed at their financing system, which, in the minds of critics, violates the social service purpose for which they are intended. Rent rebates for council house tenants will be financed in the first instance out of any surplus in the Housing Revenue Account remaining after (rebated) rents have been paid. If

---

[d]Assuming that the state is paying up its full need standard. Many are not.

there is no such surplus or the surplus is not sufficient to cover the full value of the rent rebates, then the remaining cost of the rebate will be financed by a central government subsidy equal to 75 percent of the deficiency, and a rate contribution equal to 25 percent. Rent allowances for private rental sector tenants will be financed through an 80 percent central government subsidy and a 20 percent rate contribution, although the full cost of administration must be borne by the local authority. However, if the Housing Revenue Account is still in surplus after the payment of rent rebates, then the surplus must be applied towards reducing the central government's share of the cost of rent allowances. If a surplus still remains after rent allowances are paid for, then it is divided equally between the central government and the local authority general fund.

As a result of this system, if there is no surplus in the HRA, the local authority will be required to finance a portion of the cost of nationally mandated rent rebates and rent allowances, and since it is likely to be the most needy local authorities who have the greatest cost for these purposes, and who have no surpluses, it will be their rate payers who bear the heaviest burden. If there is a surplus in the accounts, then the burden for rent rebates and rent allowances will rest not, it is argued, on the general taxpayer or even the local rate payer, but on the better-off council tenant who does not receive a rebate. To some, this type of redistribution is viewed as socially regressive since it is, in effect, a transfer of income from council house tenants (or at least better-off council house tenants) to private sector tenants. However, the scheme looks quite different if viewed as a transfer between income classes rather than tenure groups, assuming, that is, that take-up rates are reasonably high.

In the United States, much the same situation obtains in public housing: in effect, rebates for poorer tenants are paid for out of rents by less poor tenants—although since 1970, that portion of the rebates due to legislation restricting rent to 25 percent of income has been financed by operating costs subsidies from the federal government and thus the nation's taxpayers. Subsidies in federally assisted, privately owned rental housing are likewise financed through the federal tax base.

In addition to rent subsidies provided through the housing system, both countries also pay de facto housing subsidies through their public assistance systems. In the United Kingdom, supplementary benefits (the equivalent of public assistance) take account of housing need by adding the actual cost of housing to a set needs allowance in order to determine the budget requirements of a family. The family then receives supplementary benefits in the amount by which the needs budget exceeds actual income. Tenants receiving rent rebates or allowances initially had to first calculate their rebated rent as the basis for receiving supplementary benefits, but when this system proved too complex, it was changed so that the tenant applies for supplementary benefit on the basis of his full rent and, in effect, receives his rent rebate or allowance in his supplementary benefit payment.

In the United States, the public assistance system[e] in most states theoretically works much the same way as described above. A needs budget, which includes the actual cost of housing (in some states limited to a set maximum), is calculated, and a recipient is eligible for assistance if income is less than needs. In some states the needs budget includes only an average housing cost rather than actual cost. However, in many states the theoretical similarity with the U.K. system is misleading because, due to a lack of sufficient resources and/or political opposition to high public assistance cost, the standard from which public assistance is actually calculated may be lower than the needs standard or a maximum payment lower than the needs standard may be imposed.

According to a recent study by HUD, the housing component of public assistance dwarfs, at least in terms of funds spent, other governmental housing efforts:

Estimates by the Department of Health, Education and Welfare suggest, however, that of the total welfare expenditures in 1972 by State and Federal Governments, approximately $7.6 billion was used by welfare families for housing. By making further arbitrary assumptions, it was estimated that of the $7.6 billion provided to the states by the Federal Government $2.6 billion was used for housing. This highly approximate figure compares with the $2.5 billion the Federal Government allotted the same year to carry out all of its direct housing subsidy programs.[1]

There has been a great deal of interest in the United States in the possibilities of a housing allowance system that would provide subsidies directly to households rather than to houses. When President Nixon suspended the most federally assisted programs in January 1973 (including public housing), he stated that a system of housing allowances might well prove a preferable alternative. Legislation passed in 1970 mandated HUD to conduct a housing allowance experiment to determine what its consequences might be and how practical it might prove. The experiment is now underway.

Housing allowances appear quite appealing as a social service device in the American context, for they conform to the preference for providing cash rather than in-kind goods or services, and they also, when compared to present programs, enhance individual choice. Thus, consumer sovereignty rather than government planning (or interference with the market's operations) would characterize the program's operations.

---

[e]It should be noted that the public assistance systems in the two countries differ in important respects. In the United Kingdom, supplementary benefits are available to *all* families whose head is unemployed and to unemployed individuals. Family Income Supplements are available to families whose head is employed but earning a low wage. In the United States, public assistance is available to all old-aged people and to families with children if the head is unemployed or employed less than full time. However, in about 40 percent of the states benefits are available *only* to female-headed families, and not to male-headed families. There is no provision for assistance to fully employed workers. Furthermore benefits vary from state to state in the United States, whereas they are standardized throughout the United Kingdom.

Yet there are obvious problems. There is general agreement among British observers that the rental housing allowance system now in effect in the United Kingdom is workable only within the context of rent control or regulation. Otherwise, in tight markets the subsidy will simply be eaten up by higher rents. Yet, as we have seen, rent control does not exist in most U.S. cities, nor is it likely to. It is possible, however, that in response to an operating cost subsidy or some mechanism by which they can obtain a higher rent, landlords may be persuaded to accept government-controlled rents (the situation that now exists in most federal housing programs).

Yet housing allowances, even combined with rent controls, may not solve the problem of poor housing conditions, for they leave an important cause untouched. In many areas, increased demand, even if the market is not tight, will not result in improved housing conditions until landlords are able to receive a rent sufficient to derive a reasonable return on their property after it has been improved to standard condition. So the dilemma is this: increased demand with a rent-control system, which prevents rents from reaching these levels, will generate a classical shortage situation; increased demand without rent controls will likely result in higher rents without much improvement in housing conditions, unless the housing allowance (plus perhaps an operating subsidy to the landlord) is high enough to provide the landlord a reasonable return for a standard dwelling; but a housing allowance high enough to permit such a return will result in very high budgetary cost to the federal government unless the number of people eligible to receive it is limited. In that case some kind of equity problem will be inevitable.

Thus, the policy questions posed by the housing allowance alternative revolve around the question of how universal the allowance should be and how much discretion should be allowed in its expenditure. Some of the same questions are now under debate in the United Kingdom with respect to the rent-rebate and allowance system. Should the subsidy be universal or only to renters, as in the United Kingdom? Should it be given in the form of a cash payment to the household or in a form (such as a voucher or a rebate) that can only be used for housing, again as in the United Kingdom? Should it be usable for any housing unit in which the family may decide to reside or only in a unit for which the landlord agrees to accept a regulated rent? Should it be payable to a tenant living in substandard housing (as in the United Kingdom), or should it be payable only for standard housing or in such a way that landlords of substandard housing can only use the funds for repairs? Should the subsidy be means tested (as in the United Kingdom), and by what device? The British system is still too new to permit definitive conclusions based on experience, but it would behoove American policy makers to watch its performance closely, particularly as research begins to throw some light upon many of the above questions.

7 Homeownership

The strong socio-cultural preference for homeownership, combined with rising real per capital income and favorable tax policies, has lead to a steady increase in the rate of homeownership for both countries. Owner-occupancy clearly confers a substantial advantage on those who are fortunate enough to achieve it. They receive nearly absolute security of tenure, a home place that they can shape as they like to fit their own personal needs, substantial tax breaks, and rent-free accommodations while building up equity in a capital asset, which during the past several years has appreciated quickly and promises to continue to do so. Particularly during the soaring inflation of the past few years, homeownership has proven to be one of the few real hedges available to the average man. As of 1972, 62 percent of American households and 51 percent of British owned their own homes (see Table 7-1). In both countries, homeownership is focused above the median income level, although it ranges throughout the income distribution.

Both countries—although the United States more clearly than the United Kingdom—have represented homeownership, at least rhetorically, as a social good that should be available at reasonable cost to the great majority of citizens who are not poor. It has, in effect, become nearly a social right. However, in both countries there is a perception that recent rapid rises in the price of homeownership and the cost and availability of mortgage funds have threatened the possibility of attaining this "social right" for many people who legitimately aspire to it. Thus, B. Bruce Briggs quotes a U.S. Congressman, Thomas Ashley:

While the middle class may well be indifferent to the plight of the poor, it can no longer ignore the fact that they themselves are being priced out of the housing market.

Testifying before the House Banking and Currency Committee [sic] in early 1970, HUD Secretary Romney stated that to afford the median-priced home then being offered for sale ($27,000) without unreasonably stretching its budget, a family needed an income of nearly $14,000. It's a remarkable statistic and, despite modest decreases in financing cost since then, it is not much improved today.

The housing crisis is clearly spreading to the once comfortable middle class, and if land and construction costs continue to increase faster than personal income, the crisis will surely intensify.[a]

---

[a]B. Bruce Briggs, "The Cost of Housing," *The Public Interest* Summer 1973, No. 32, p. 34. Briggs goes on to argue that, in fact, house prices have not risen faster than income and that the "crisis" is exaggerated. Nonetheless Ashley's statement—and Briggs' article debunking what it represents—demonstrate the political impact of rising house prices.

Table 7-1
Owner-Occupancy in the United Kingdom, 1972

Weekly Income (£)	Percent of All Homeowners	Percent of Income Class Owning Home
Under 10	2.6	15.7
10-15	5.4	29.6
15-20	4.6	35.9
20-25	5.1	35.9
25-30	5.8	37.6
30-35	6.5	38.9
35-40	8.2	43.0
40-45	9.2	54.2
45-50	8.5	53.4
50-60	15.0	59.9
60-80	16.3	61.4
Over 80	12.8	74.8

Source: U.K., *Family Expenditure Survey, Report for 1972*, HMSO, 1973, p. 14. The pattern in the United States would be much the same.

In the United Kingdom, the dismay at soaring house prices has been even more vigorously expressed. During a House of Commons debate, Anthony Crosland observed:

> ... the new home buyer has been hit by a vicious one-two combination punch. First he has been hit by the crazy rise in house prices. ... As if this were not enough he has been hit by the ballooning mortgage rate. ... It is now almost impossible for the wage earner on average earnings to buy a home of his own. In 1970, if he spent just under 30 percent—or to be exact 29.8 percent—of his income on mortgage, he could buy an average new house. After tax relief this was just possible, although clearly a strain. But it would now cost a worker on average earnings half his income, so that is clearly out of the question.[b]

---

[b]U.K., Hansard, House of Commons, 6th November 1973, 811. Politicians apparently believe that no one will purchase a house below the median or average price, a logical fallacy that improves their argument, perhaps, but not our understanding. Note that Crosland appears to believe as well that home buyers will buy only *new* homes.

House Purchase Prices

In fact, while house prices in the United States have increased faster than inflation, they have not, at least through 1972, increased faster than the rise in per capita disposable income. From 1967 to 1972, the average cost of purchasing a home, according to the consumer price index, rose by 29.4 percent. During the same time, the entire consumer price index (a measure of inflation) increased by 25.3 percent and per capita disposable income increased by 39.1 percent.[1] Compared to the U.K. experience, the increase in house prices has been quite moderate. From 1968 to 1973, the average dwelling price increased in the United Kingdom by 125 percent—from £4,344 to £9,733. During the same time, retail prices throughout the economy increased by 44 percent and disposable income per capita by 65 percent. The great rise in prices came during 1973 when house prices increased more than 35 percent, from £7,374 to £9,733.[c]

What accounts for these increases? It appears that in both countries the sharply increasing cost of land has been a major culprit. In the United States, the price of a square foot of land of new housing sites rose by 83 percent between 1967 and 1972. During the same period, average lot size fell by 12 percent, so the cost of land per new dwelling unit rose by about 61 percent. However, in 1971, the average site-value ratio for new homes was only 18.3 percent—an increase from about 15 percent in 1967. Thus, it is unlikely that the increase in land costs accounted for more than about one-third of the increase in house prices.[2] Or, put in another way, a decrease in land prices by one-third would reduce house purchase prices by between 6 and 7 percent.

In the United Kingdom, the average price per plot for new housing has increased over a four-year period from £828 in 1969 to £2,589 in 1973—an increase of 212 percent. The average site-value ratio for new housing rose substantially from 17.1 percent in 1969 to 25.9 percent in 1973. Still, while average new dwelling prices increased by £5,000 between 1969 and 1973, land prices increased by less than £1,800, thereby accounting for about 36 percent of the increase. A decrease in land prices by one-third would decrease house purchase prices by between 8 and 9 percent.[3]

In both countries, while construction costs (materials, wages, overhead—including profit—and equipment) have been rising more slowly than land costs, nonetheless in absolute terms they account for a much higher proportion of the

---

[c]U.K., Department of Environment, *Housing and Construction Statistics*, HMSO, No. 7, 3rd Quarter, 1973, p. 45. House prices in the United States also rose substantially during 1973. Unfortunately we do not have data on the extent of these increases; it is possible therefore that the seemingly moderate increases in U.S. prices over a five-year period compared to the United Kingdom may be understated.

increase in house purchase prices than do land costs.[d] Yet policy proposals designed to reduce house prices have, particularly in the United Kingdom, focused on reducing the price of land. The previous Conservative Government proposed to increase the supply of land by releasing land in Green Belt areas for building and by imposing a land-hoarding tax to discourage land speculators from withholding land from the market. The Labour Government is committed to nationalization of land in the path of urban development as a means of increasing the supply of land available for house building and assuring a substantial portion of any profit from change of use of the land accrues to the community.

Homeownership Costs

Of course the actual house purchase price represents only one item in the cost of homeownership. In 1972, monthly homeownership costs in the United States were 40.1 percent higher than they had been in 1967. The breakdown in these costs and the percentage increase in each component are listed in Table 7-2.

Unfortunately similar data is not readily available for the United Kingdom,

Table 7-2
Cost of Homeownership in the United States, 1972

	Percent of Total Cost	Percent Increase in Component Since 1967	Percent of Total Increase Accounted for by Component
House Purchase	39.5	29.4	30.9
Mortgage Interest Repayments[a]	23.5	52.6	27.9
Maintenance and Repairs	19.7	41.0	22.9
Property Taxes[a]	13.7	50.6	15.7
Property Insurance	3.6	25.0	2.5

[a]These costs are somewhat overstated because they are deductible from gross income for income tax purposes.
Source: Derived from data in U.S., Department of Housing and Urban Development, *Housing in the Seventies* (Washington, D.C.: HUD, 1973), pp. 8-10.

---

[d]In the United Kingdom, the cost of construction materials rose 43 percent between 1969 and 1973, while wages for construction workers rose by 75 percent (U.K., Department of Environment, *Housing and Construction Statistics*, No. 7, 1973, p. 2), while in the U.S. construction material costs rose 39 percent between 1967 and 1972, while wages rose 44 percent (U.S., Department of Housing and Urban Development, *Housing in the Seventies* [Washington, D.C.: HUD, 1973], p. 8-15).

but there, as in the United States, the rise in mortgage interest cost as well as the actual house purchase price have contributed to increases in the cost of home ownership. Between 1968 and 1973, the mortgage rate jumped from 7.625 percent to 11 percent and, in response to higher purchase prices, the average amount of the mortgage loan doubled. In 1969, the average income of new mortgagors was £1,762 or 104 percent of average annual household income, while in 1973 it was £2,923 or nearly 120 percent of average income.[4]

Mortgage Costs and Institutions

The cost and difficulty of obtaining mortgages is a major problem in both countries, where public policy has viewed easy mortgage money at low interest rates as a form of social service. The United Kingdom in particular has found it difficult to cope with spiralling mortgage prices. The predominant mortgage lending institution in the United Kingdom is the building society, which attracts deposits from small investors and loans them for mortgages. Local authorities also may make direct mortgage loans to home purchasers at the rate set by the Public Works Loan Board (roughly the market rate) and, in some cases, they may guarantee building society mortgages. Building societies account for about 90 percent of new mortgage loans, local authorities account for another 7 to 8 percent, and insurance companies the remainder.

Local authority mortgages are not subsidized but are likely to be at a higher loan-value ratio (100 percent mortgages are available) than are building society mortgages. The local authority role is more a supplementary social service one, providing larger loans to less sound risks than do the building societies.

The cost of mortgages are somewhat offset for most borrowers (in both countries) because tax laws enable them to deduct the amount of mortgage interest they pay during the year from taxable income. However, this deduction provides the greatest assistance to the wealthiest and the least, or none at all, to the most needy. In 1968, the British introduced an option mortgage scheme that allowed mortgagors to choose between a mortgage at market rates with the tax deduction or a mortgage at interest rates 2 to 3 percent below market level without a tax deduction. For those who chose the latter scheme, the government made up the difference between the lower interest rate and the market rate by a direct subsidy to the building society making the loan.

The option was available to any mortgagor as a matter of right. Generally it provided for equal treatment between borrowers paying standard rate income tax (for a family of four, 30 percent of income between £1,115 and £6,115) who chose the tax deduction and borrowers below the income tax threshold (£115) who chose the lower interest rate. Nonetheless, borrowers whose income put them in a tax bracket above the standard rate (in excess of £6,115 for a family of four) continued to be advantaged over either group. However, less than

5 percent of all households are in this category. In 1972, nearly 21 percent of all building society mortgages were on this option scheme, which is up sharply from 7 percent in 1970 and 9 percent in 1971.[5] Nearly two-thirds of these option mortgages were accompanied by a local authority guarantee designed to encourage building societies to accept greater risks than they have been traditionally accustomed to.

In the United States, a program of subsidized mortgages for low- and moderate-income families is available to mortgagors purchasing a home under Section 235 of the Housing Act of 1968. This program—a companion of the rental subsidy program described in Chapter 4—provides a very deep subsidy, but because it is tied to houses built or sold under a specific and limited federal program, the number of households receiving assistance from it has been quite limited. The buyer of a Section 235 home obtains an FHA-insured mortgage at a rate at or below the maximum FHA interest rate[e] from a private mortgage lender. He must make monthly payments of 20 percent of his monthly income *or* an amount necessary to retire the mortgage based on a 1 percent annual rate of interest, whichever is greater. The federal government subsidizes the rest of the mortgage repayment to the private lender. From 1968 to 1972, nearly 400,000 home buyers were subsidized through this mechanism. The program was suspended by President Nixon in January 1973. It has since been reinstated, but it is apparently being slowly phased out of existence.

Fluctuations in mortgage interest rates are more politically sensitive in the United Kingdom than in the United States because the U.K. mortgage employs a variable interest rate rather than a constant rate fixed at the time the loan is made as is the case in the United States. Thus, a change of interest rates in the United Kingdom affects all homeowners making mortgage payments and not solely newly negotiated mortgages. Obviously this creates a great deal of uncertainty for mortgagors as well as resentment when the interest rates are rising as they were from 1972 to 1974.

The variable interest rate exists partly because during times of rising interest rates, building societies require increased repayments from existing mortgages to enable them to maintain their lending activity since deposits fall as other investment opportunities become more attractive.[f] At present there is nearly no secondary market for mortgages and little governmental intervention to ensure a stable flow of mortgage funds, although proposals to deal with this problem have been widely discussed. In 1971 to 1972, a surfeit of inflow lead to a large increase in the number and value of mortgage loans, which thus helped to increase the demand for and price of housing. As interest rates rose throughout the economy in 1973 and 1974, building society deposits dropped, and

---

[e]The maximum FHA interest rate is usually slightly below market rate.

[f]But according to Della Nevitt (interview with the author, April 30, 1974) the usual response of mortgagors is to refinance their loan by extending the repayment period rather than to increase monthly payments.

mortgage money became very difficult to obtain. The Conservative Government's intervention consisted of a £15 million grant to building societies to provide them with additional lendable funds plus the placing of a limit on the interest rate payable by the building societies' chief competitor, commercial savings banks, in an effort to put a stop to disintermediation. The Labour Government immediately provided a loan of £100 million to the building societies and promised further loans in an effort to avert increases—which would be highly damaging politically—in the mortgage interest rate.

In the United States, depository institutions also form the backbone of the mortgage market with savings and loan associations and mutual savings banks now holding about 65 percent of all mortgage loans outstanding and commercial banks 15 percent. Insurance companies account for another 10 percent.[6] In terms of new loans *originated* in 1973, the savings and loans associations and mutual savings banks accounted for 51 percent, commercial banks 23 percent, and mortgage companies (non-depository institutions) 20 percent. Traditionally the depository institutions face the same type of problems in times of rising interest rates as do the British building societies; indeed the problem is intensified by statutory maximums regulating the interest rates which thrift institutions (savings and loans and mutual savings banks) can pay on deposits.

However, the governmental response to the credit constriction problem has been more innovative, although not overwhelmingly successful, in the United States. Several governmental institutions exist whose purpose is to channel necessary funds into the mortgage market when rising interest rates threaten to reduce the volume of mortgage credit. These include:

The Federal Home Loan Bank system (FHLB), which makes advances or short-term loans to member savings and loan associations when their deposits are falling. To finance its operations, the FHLB sells its consolidated debentures in the securities market.

Secondary mortgage market institutions—such as the Federal National Mortgage Association (FNMA), the Federal Home Loan Mortgage Corporation (FHLMC) and the Government National Mortgage Association (GHMA)—which purchase mortgages from the originating lending institutions in order to assure availability of new mortgage credit.

In addition (and far transcending in historical importance) to this government role in stabilizing the mortgage market, the federal government through the Federal Housing Administration (FHA) has, since 1934, provided mortgage insurance or guarantees backing up private loans. The loans must be less than a maximum amount ($33,000)[g] and the property mortgaged has to meet minimum standards. In addition, the risk underwritten by the government must be

---

[g]This figure was raised to $45,000 by the Housing and Community Development Act of 1974.

an economically sound one, although since 1968 the economic soundness criteria has been relaxed to encourage greater availability of mortgage money in inner-city areas. FHA-insured loans cannot exceed a maximum interest rate set by legislation (usually about .5 to 1 percent below market rates for conventional loans, and the borrower must pay an additional .5 percent insurance premium.[h] The primary direct benefit to the borrower, (besides the fact that lenders are more willing to make loans in a near riskless situation) is the easy terms—the low down payment and long repayment period. FHA loans normally cover 95 percent of purchase price but can cover nearly 100 percent; the normal repayment period is thirty years. Since 1935, nearly 20 percent of all mortgages have been FHA insured. Since most of the FHA loans have been for moderately priced housing, a much higher portion of that market has made use of FHA-insured mortgages.[7]

Consumer Protection

Traditionally the purchase of a house was in both countries carried on under the doctrine of "caveat emptor." The strains between this doctrine and a social service philosophy with respect to housing are obvious, particularly in an era when homeownership is widespread and ranges throughout the income distribution. Nonetheless actions to protect home buyers from the effects of purchasing an inferior product have been rather recent in the United Kingdom and are still in the beginning stages in the United States.

In the United Kingdom, the National Housebuilders Registration Council (NHBRC) was set up in the mid-1960s, under government prodding, to institute a warranty system for new houses. Under the scheme, buyers who purchase a new home from a builder registered with NHBRC receive a warranty for the first two years against defects in the home that result from the builder's failure to comply with the Council's specification of standards of workmanship and materials. The full cost of remedying any such defect must be borne by the builder. In addition, the purchaser is insured against damage due to "major" defects in the load-bearing structure from the third to the tenth year to a maximum of £10,000 per dwelling. The cost of repairing these major defects is borne not by the builder but by an insurance policy negotiated through NHBRC on behalf of purchasers. The home buyer must pay an insurance fee averaging around £12 at the time of purchase.

Builders are not required to join the NHBRC, but it is estimated that the great majority of them have done so. Prior to receiving registration, a builder

---

[h]Although when the maximum FHA rate is substantially below market rate, lenders recoup the difference by charging discount points that the seller, in arranging financing, must pay in a lump sum normally added on to the price of the house in the form of an increased down payment.

with houses under construction must satisfy the Council that its houses meet the NHBRC's standards. It must submit its plans for construction to the Council at least fourteen days before beginning and must agree to build to the detailed standards of the NHBRC. The Council employs its own staff of inspectors and attempts to make on-site visits to houses under construction at three week intervals to assure that standards are being met. Builders whose work is not up to the standards may be de-registered, which puts them at a severe competitive disadvantage since they then cannot offer the ten year protection to their purchasers.

In the United States, the National Association of Homebuilders (NAHB), the trade organization for the nation's home builders, has within the past year decided to institute a similar system. It has done so in response to growing demands for government action protecting home buyers against expensive defects. The problem was particularly severe in federally assisted homeownership programs where low- and moderate-income purchasers were often inexperienced first-time home buyers with very limited resources. While NAHB adoption of the NHBRC system will be a significant improvement for purchasers of new homes, it will not provide protection for buyers of existing homes, which is the area where the worst abuses take place.

Summary

Homeownership has been accepted and encouraged as a social good for the non-poor household in both countries. However the rising costs of homeownership due to increases in both house purchase prices and mortgage interest rates are now perceived to threaten attainment of this goal by many middle- and working-class citizens who aspire to it. Although a recent problem, it is therefore one of pre-eminent political importance. Policy responses as yet have been tentative and uncertain, although the most obvious points of intervention appear to be mortgage market institutions (particularly in the United States) and the land market.

8 Maintenance of the Housing Stock

Code Enforcement

In both the United Kingdom and the United States, enforcement of minimum housing standards represents the first social service function—indeed the first function of any sort—that government took upon itself in the housing area. Legislation dating back to 1868 establishes the right and duty of local authorities in the United Kingdom to establish public health standards for housing and to demolish unfit housing. In the United States, housing codes began to appear at the end of the nineteenth century in a few cities, but it has only been within the last 25 years that they have become a common feature. Unlike the United Kingdom, local governments in the United States are not required to have minimum housing standards (although they are highly encouraged by the federal government to do so, sometimes to the point of coercion), and housing codes that do exist are legislated by individual localities rather than the national government. In fact, the administration of housing codes represents the primary—and in many cases the sole—housing function performed by most American cities.

In the United Kingdom, local authorities have a statutory duty set by national legislation to inspect the houses in their district from time to time to determine whether any houses are unfit. If a house is found to be "unfit for human habitation" the local authority has four options, one of which it must choose:

1. If the house can be repaired at reasonable cost, it can issue a repair notice upon the owner. If the owner does not comply, the local authority can carry out the work itself and recover the cost from the owner.
2. It can issue a demolition order and demolish the house.
3. It can issue a closing order requiring the house be closed and vacated but not demolished. A closing order might be issued if it is inexpedient to demolish the house because of the possible effect of demolition on other buildings or if only a portion of the building (a room or a flat) is unfit. No compensation is paid for the demolition or closing of an unfit unit.
4. It can purchase the house (at site value) and repair the house so that it is capable of providing accommodation which is "adequate for the time being." This is variously called the "patched house" or "deferred demolition" procedure. The local authority receives an Exchequer grant to help bring the

house up to the required standard, then uses the house as part of the council stock until it is demolished at a later date.

The local authority may also determine that an entire area of houses is unfit or so badly arranged as to be dangerous or hazardous to the health of the inhabitants of the area. In this case, it can declare the area a clearance area, acquire the site (paying site value to owners of unfit property), demolish the buildings—or use the deferred demolition procedure described above—clear the area and then redevelop the area. This is quite similar to the American urban renewal program.

Of the four remedies, demolition appears to be the most common and the great majority of demolition activity occurs in clearance areas. In 1973, there were 60,721 demolitions of which 52,729 were in clearance areas (included in this latter figure were 5,898 houses that were not unfit). In the same year, 4,677 unfit houses outside of clearance areas were closed but not demolished. As for repairs orders, Daniel Mandelker observes that "while a substantial volume of repair has been carried out under this statute, it has not primarily been viewed as a housing improvement remedy. One reason is that a finding of unfitness cannot usually be made unless the building is beyond a state in which repair is feasible."[1]

British minimum housing standards, at least as expressed through the definition of unfit housing, are not nearly as rigid or detailed as American housing codes (in fact in some ways the British statute and the common effect of its usage—demolition—bear closer resemblance to American demolition statutes than to American housing codes). The standard of fitness, as defined in the Housing Act of 1957, leaves a great deal of room for administrative discretion:

In determining for any of the purposes of this Act, whether a house is unfit for human habitation, regard shall be had to its condition in respect of the following matters, that is to say—

a. repairs
b. stability
c. freedom from damp
cc. internal arrangement
d. natural lighting
e. ventilation
f. water supply
g. drainage and sanitary conveniences
h. facilities for preparation and cooking of food and for the disposal of waste water.

And the house shall be deemed to be unfit as aforesaid if, and only if, it is so far defective in one or more of said matters that it is not reasonably suitable for occupation in that condition.[2]

In the United States, housing codes, although they vary from locality to locality, are much more rigid and seemingly leave much less room for discretion in their application (in fact this is largely illusory). Unlike the British equivalent, which deals with fitness and unfitness in a rather broad sense, American codes aim at achieving minimum housing standards in a multitude of specific categories through a continual process of inspection and repair. That at least is the theory.

The categories regulated by housing codes fall into three basic areas:

1. The facilities that must exist in the structure (toilet, bath, sink, and so forth);
2. The level of maintenance and service to be provided, including both structural and sanitary maintenance, leaks in the roof, broken banisters, cracks in the wall, and so forth;
3. Occupancy standards, including the site of dwelling units and of rooms of different types and the permitted number of people per room.[a]

The mere existence of housing codes in American cities is a very recent phenomena. Less than twenty years ago, in 1956, the U.S. Housing and Home Finance Agency estimated only 56 cities in the entire country had housing codes.[b] In 1968, a survey by the National Commission on Urban Problems counted 4,904 local governments with codes, still less than 30 percent of all urban communities in the United States, but a startling increase in barely twelve years time. The advance is even more striking for larger cities over 50,000, 85 percent of which had codes.[3]

The great proliferation of housing codes is almost entirely due to federal government "encouragement." In 1954, Congress passed legislation requiring that communities wishing to receive urban renewal subsidies for slum clearance and redevelopment[c] must first adopt a "Workable Program," one element of which consisted of adequate local codes and ordinances. In 1964 and 1965, the

---

[a]Occupancy standards in the United Kingdom are separate from the regulation of "unfit houses." Overcrowding is defined as the occupancy of the same sleeping room by two children of opposite sex over the age of 10 and not living together as man and wife. There are also standards relating to the minimum necessary floor space per person. Overcrowding is illegal and is punishable by a fine of £5 plus £2 per each day the condition persists after conviction. Houses in multiple occupation—that is, occupied by more than one family (usually rooming houses)—are also subject to regulation. If the local authority decides that the house is in such a condition (either with respect to overcrowding or provision of amenities and facilities) that the safety, welfare, or health of persons living in the house is endangered, it may issue a control order authorizing it to take over control and management of the house.

[b]Building codes cover the structural requirements of new buildings.

[c]Urban renewal subsidies cover two-thirds of the difference between the local government's cost of acquiring and clearing the property and the price it receives from selling for redevelopment according to its approved urban renewal plan. Legislation passed in 1974 provided for the phased termination of the urban renewal program and its "workable program" requirement. It was replaced by a block grant program, which will provide funds to cities with relatively few guidelines or restrictions upon its use.

act was amended so that the "Workable Program" must include not only a minimum standards housing code, but also an effective program of enforcement to achieve compliance with codes. Of the nearly 5,000 housing codes existing in 1968, HUD has estimated more than 3,000 are *directly* attributable to workable program provision.[4] In 1965, Congress further encouraged the development of housing codes by passing the Federally Assisted Code Enforcement program that provided cities with two-thirds of the cost of setting up and administering a comprehensive housing code.

Despite the recent proliferation of housing codes, it is widely agreed that they have in fact done little to enforce minimum housing standards. The reasons for this are many:

1. Most cities have inadequate funding and inadequate staff for administering their housing codes, and enforcement is not usually considered a high priority activity.
2. Only the city, not an individual occupant, can bring suit for violation of a local housing code.
3. Enforcement remedies are generally weak. If the owner does not comply, he can be brought to court where only criminal penalties are available. Fines are usually quite small and many landlords merely accept them as an addition to their operating cost and as being far less costly than actually keeping their buildings up to code. Jail sentences may be provided for in the code but are rarely imposed.
4. In many cases, the owner does not have the wherewithal to make the necessary repairs. The building simply does not generate a sufficient rental income to cover its costs and allow for a reasonable return on investment; many landlords try to meet this by decreasing maintenance and repairs expenditures rather than increasing them as code enforcement requires.

Thus, strict housing code enforcement may lead to abandonment and increased blight (since demolition is a much less common and more difficult remedy in the United States than the United Kingdom). As the National Commission on Urban Problems observed:

Commission studies on this point have led to the conclusion (at least in Boston and the Boston housing code is less stringent than many) that strict enforcement on a mass basis would lead to mass abandonment of properties by their owners and/or higher rents with resultant occupant displacement. When mass enforcement is applied to properties that have been heavily milked and are under rent control as in the Brownsville section of Brooklyn, New York, mass abandonment will occur if housing is *not* in short supply. In Philadelphia, without rent control, strict code enforcement has developed thousands of vacant, dilapidated houses, most of which are tax delinquent.... Buildings left vacant, especially in the poorer areas of a city, are vulnerable to vandalism and arson. If a city's powers are weak or its procedures cumbersome for demolishing vacant structures, it fires the threat of creating new blighting influences by housing code enforcement action that produces in an end product a vacant vandalized structure.[5]

In some cases the difficulty in achieving adequate housing code enforcement has led cities to search for new remedies. By 1970, seven states had enacted receivership laws allowing their cities to place units with code violations in the receivership of a municipal officer. The receiver would apply rent receipts to correcting code violations, until such time as the violations were corrected, when the receivership would end. New York City and Chicago have both made substantial use of this device. New York and a few other cities have also utilized a program in which the city makes repairs for code violations and places a lien on rents in order to pay the cost. In both cases, it has been found that full application of the rent revenue to repairs is often insufficient to bring the building to code standards, and the city must contribute funds of its own. Chicago allows receivers to sell receivership certificates, which are interest bearing, negotiable, and represent a first lien on the property. Clearly any program that applies full rents towards repairs will not be enthusiastically received by the mortgagee who will no longer receive his monthly principal and interest payments. As a result, it is charged, both programs have contributed to the abandonment problem.

From his survey of Baltimore, Stegman concludes:

As a practical matter, the code cannot be universally enforced without some sort of subsidy. According to our data, the median expenditure required to bring the substandard inventory into compliance is $1000, whereas actual expenditures which are incurred as a result of enforcement average only about $200. If a policy of vigorous unsubsidized enforcement were pursued, widespread boarding up would no doubt result.[6]

And Grigsby usefully places code enforcement in perspective as a device for combatting slum housing. Observing that "it is clear that at present code enforcement programs are frequently not simply ineffectual but actually perverse in the impact on housing quality and urban environment," he then argues:

The lesson of Baltimore and Philadelphia would seem to be that for enforcement to be effective, an environment must be created which is conducive to maintenance and investment by investors, owner-occupants, and tenants, not simply in response to enforcement, but prior to the use of legal sticks.... Creation of an adequate economic environment in the inner city requires a host of housing and non-housing interventions. Within the sphere of housing, a few of these interventions seem obvious. One is vastly improved city services. A second is greater focus on improvement of the exterior of the dwelling units, because of the effect that this has on peoples' perceptions of the environment. A third is large-scale transfers of ownership to persons and groups who can and will respond to code enforcement and who have the resources to maintain and manage dwelling units. A fourth is subsidies to either the demander or the suppliers of housing. And fifth, and finally, is some attention to landlord-tenant relations. None of these necessary supporting programs is without cost.[7]

Improvements, Repairs, and Rehabilitation

During the last decade rehabilitation has been viewed in both the United States and United Kingdom as an increasingly desirable alternative to clearance and redevelopment. The United Kingdom in particular, with a high portion of old houses in viable neighborhoods and a scarcity of land, has adopted this approach as much less socially divisive and much less expensive in terms of investment than a massive program of new building.

Improvement grants originated in the United Kingdom with the Housing Act of 1949, but it was not until the late 1960s that they became an important element of public policy. At that time, the government announced its intention that "within a total of public investment in housing at about the level it has now reached, a greater share should go to the improvement of older housing."[8] As can be seen in Table 8-1, in 1966, only 117,000 improvement grants were approved. This figure more than tripled to 371,000 in 1972,[9] and was 40,000 more than the total number of new units built that year.

As Table 8-1 indicates, the grants are available to owners of all dwelling units (including local authorities) without regard to tenure, income, or location. Recipients must contribute 50 percent of the cost themselves and the local authority contributes the other 50 percent up to a set maximum (although in certain areas a 75 percent grant is available). The central government, in turn, pays 75 percent of the local authority's cost. Recipients may apply to the local

Table 8-1
House Improvement Grants in Great Britain, 1966-1973 (in Thousands)

	Private Owner-Occupiers	Private Rental	Local Authority	Total
1966	56	27	34	117
1968	59	28	41	128
1969	57	27	40	124
1970	80	43	60	183
1971	93	53	90	236
1972	157	76	137	371
1973	186	76	188	450

Source: U.K., Central Statistical Office, *Social Trends*, HMSO, No. 4, 1973 p. 158; and U.K., Department of Environment, *Housing and Construction Statistics*, HMSO, No. 7, 4th Quarter, 1973, p. 38.

authority for a loan to cover their share of the cost, but only 15,000 of these were approved in 1972 out of 208,000 made to private owners.

There are basically two types of grants, a standard grant and a discretionary grant. The standard grant is available as a right to any owner who qualifies. It covers installation of any or all of the following amenities: a fixed bath or shower; a hot and cold water supply at a fixed bath or shower; a wash hand basin; a hot and cold water supply at a wash hand basin; a sink; a hot and cold water supply at a sink; and a water closet (toilet). The maximum available standard grant is £200, and when the work is completed the unit must possess all the above amenities and have a life of at least fifteen years.

The discretionary grant is not provided as a right but according to the judgment of the local authority. It can be used for an improvement (of almost any kind), for conversion of large units into several smaller ones, and, since 1969, for repairs incidental to the improvement or necessary to make the improvement fully effective.[d] The maximum discretionary grant is £1,000.

Legislation passed in 1964 permitted local authorities to identify areas suitable for comprehensive improvement and to compel owners to provide the standard amenities to every tenanted house in the area. This authority was sparsely used and was abolished in 1969. The 1969 legislation also provided for the designation of General Improvement Areas that would be eligible for grants for neighborhood and environmental improvement.

The results of the improvement grant strategy have been mixed. Standard grants have undoubtedly been used to install basic amenities in many houses, but these now account for less than 20 percent of all grants, as opposed to more than 60 percent in 1961. The discretionary improvement grants have been monopolized by the local authorities (43 percent in 1972) and owner-occupiers (39 percent) rather than private landlords. In 1972, excluding conversion grants, only 15 percent of discretionary grants were awarded to the private rental sector even though 54 percent of all unfit units were in that sector.[10] To some extent this must be due to the grant structure that discourages poor people or people without ready capital from making use of the grants, since they must bear 50 percent of the cost themselves. Many of the worst housing units are indeed owned by elderly or impecunious landlords. On the other hand, there is no income limit for eligibility, so relatively wealthy owner-occupiers can use the grant to pay for 50 percent of the cost of repairs they may well have made in any case.

Those improvement grants that do reach the private rental sector, particularly in the London area, have too often resulted in displacement rather than improvement for sitting tenants, particularly in the furnished sector where security of tenure did not exist until the Labour Government instituted it in 1974. Owners, including property companies who have recently purchased old housing in need of improvement, use the grants to improve or convert existing

---
[d]But in no case can more than half the grant be used for repairs.

low-income units into luxury units, usually for sale. Alternatively, existing owners may use the improvement grant to improve the value of their property prior to sale. Given the serious housing shortage in areas such as London, the previous tenants are faced with great difficulty in obtaining comparable housing and may even be rendered homeless.

The 1973 White Paper, *Better Homes: The Next Priorities*[11] proposed several remedies to attack the misuse of improvement grants. These included prohibiting grants to owners of highly valued properties, requiring that recipients of improvement grants must keep the property available for renting at registered rents for at least three years after the grant, and providing a penalty for recipients who sold the improved property within that period. The White Paper proposals were embodied in an act that was being debated in Parliament just before the 1974 General Election was called. The Labour Government has adopted this approach and even strengthened these provisions by introducing legislation extending the time period to five years and seven years within housing action areas.

In the United States, rehabilitation came to be viewed in some quarters during the 1960s as nearly a panacea for low-income inner-city housing. As in the United Kingdom, it was seen as an alternative to the slum clearance and urban renewal program that, between 1949 and 1967, demolished 400,000 dwelling units, almost all of them occupied by low- and moderate-income households, and replaced them with 107,000 units, only 42,000 of which were for low- and moderate-income families.[12] Rehabilitation would provide decent housing for low- and moderate-income families without displacing them or destroying neighborhoods; it would promote social cohesion rather than social divisiveness; it would be quicker, easier, and cheaper than clearance and new construction; and it could involve the inner-city residents themselves in developing construction skills they could put to permanent use. Or so its proponents have argued.

In 1964 and 1965, Congress passed legislation designed to encourage residential rehabilitation efforts. Unlike the British equivalents, these programs are limited to specific geographic areas and to low- or moderate-income families. And they are discretionary. The Section 115 rehabilitation grant program provides grants up to $3,500 for owner-occupants living in designated urban renewal areas whose income is less than $3,000 per year. The Section 312 rehabilitation loan program provides subsidized loans of up to $12,000 per dwelling unit ($17,400 in high-cost areas) to owner-occupants or landlords in urban renewal areas or areas designated by the city as having a substantial number of structures in need of rehabilitation. The loans are for a maximum of twenty years at a 3 percent interest rate, and priority is given to applicants whose income does not exceed 135 percent of the public housing income limits for the area. In 1966, an additional program (221 h) provided direct below market interest rate loans (1 percent) to non-profit groups to purchase and rehabilitate housing for sale to low-income families. This program was merged into the homeownership interest subsidy programs passed in 1968 and described in Chapter 7.

While the American programs are structured to prevent some of the problems their British cousins have suffered from, they in fact go much too far in limiting eligibility for the grant. Worse, far too little money has been made available. From inception in 1965 until 1971, the three programs described above have resulted in only 55,000 rehabilitated units. During the same time 2,574,000 properties were improved, repaired, or altered through unsubsidized loans obtained on the private market and insured by the FHA.[13] Unfortunately these insured loans cannot provide adequate assistance for owners of most inner-city property in need of rehabilitation.

Partly because of the inadequate financial structure, rehabilitation has not met the high promises set for it. It has often proved quite costly, sometimes more costly even than new construction; in many cases substantial rent increases are necessitated. As in London, rehabilitation in American cities has often caused dislocation and relocation problems, both because most substantial improvements require the unit to be vacated and because of the rent increases that often follow. And, for both the above reasons, rehabilitation has often called forth community opposition leading to social divisiveness rather than cohesion, albeit undoubtedly on a much smaller scale than would clearance and redevelopment.

9 The Role of Local Government

One of the most consistent themes in our comparison is that the social service approach to housing is institutionalized at the local government level in the United Kingdom to a much greater extent that it is in the United States. Local authorities in the United Kingdom are in a broad sense assigned the responsibility of meeting the housing needs of their citizens. This is not the case in the United States where only a relatively few housing-related functions are recognized as falling clearly within the responsibility of city government.

Thus, it is the local authority that, at least in theory, bears the major portion of the responsibility for carrying out a social service approach to implement the social service goal of assuring that all British citizens are decently housed. How well do local authorities in fact perform this task?

The Housing Role

It appears that until quite recently most authorities indeed saw their role as much more restrictive than performance of a broad social service goal. They identified with the public sector and saw their main task as the production, allocation, and management of council housing. However, several recent official studies and reports have criticized this limited view and have urged local authorities to create truly comprehensive housing services. The first of these, the Seebohm Committee report, observed:

At present housing departments are primarily concerned with building, allocating and managing council houses, clearing slums, and taking measures to abate overcrowding, although some are endeavoring to do more. All housing authorities should, we consider, take a comprehensive and extended view of their responsibilities to meet the housing needs of their areas. In particular they should be generally concerned with assisting a family to obtain and keep adequate accommodation whether it be in the council house sector or not.[1]

And, as J.B. Cullingworth comments:

Part of the problem of housing management arises from what might be called the "waiting list philosophy." This has two very serious shortcomings. First it implies that the local housing authority is concerned only with those who want, apply for and are considered eligible for council housing. Those who want other types of housing (or housing which the council does not provide); those who do not apply (perhaps because they think it is a "waste of time" to do so) and those who are rejected as ineligible, are ignored. The local authority has thus little or no idea how far they are meeting the needs of their area and, even less, how far the needs of their area are being met by other agencies of housing provision. Secondly it implies that the role of the local authority is to actively meet the needs only of those at the 'top' of their list; the rest must wait.

All this stems from the way in which public authority housing has developed in Britain. Rather than being responsible for surveying the total needs of their areas and for ensuring that sufficient provision is made by all the appropriate agencies, local authorities have been predominantly concerned with the building and management of houses for those whose needs they recognise.[2]

The Institute of Housing Managers, the professional body representing local housing officials, has accepted this criticism and has urged its members to move towards a comprehensive view of local authority housing responsibilities.

It is being increasingly recognized that the best way for a local authority to meet the housing requirements of its area is to employ and co-ordinate all available agencies; and action taken to cater for the total needs of an area will produce much information about housing conditions in all sectors which otherwise might be missed. Local housing authorities, the only bodies with complete oversight of the housing problems in their areas, have many and varied powers, and by operating comprehensive housing services they can make the best use of these powers, locally to help people to solve their housing problems in the way most suited to their particular needs and resources, and nationally to improve the total housing stock and environment.[3]

The Institute envisions the following duties for a fully comprehensive housing service to be provided by a local housing authority:

To consider the housing conditions of the district with respect to the provision of housing accommodation.

To provide housing accommodation through the erection and acquisition of houses, or through the conversion, alteration or improvement of properties acquired by the council.

To acquire, develop or dispose of land and houses for housing purposes and to agree arrangements for overspill.

To arrange for inspections to be carried out from time to time to ensure that there are satisfactory standards of repair, maintenance and sanitation in housing accommodation.

To exercise powers and duties as to clearance areas and orders, unfit houses, overcrowding, houses in multiple occupation, improvement of dwellings and other general powers and duties relating thereto, by:

a. securing the effective treatment of unfit houses, including making of demolition and closing orders;
b. arranging for the inspection of housing to secure the detection and abatement of overcrowding;
c. providing financial assistance to persons wishing to improve their houses;
d. arranging improvements to groups of houses and tenement accommodation;
e. exercising powers in relation to the designation of general improvement areas.

To provide temporary accommodation for those in urgent need through homelessness or emergency.

To exercise powers in relation to housing associations, housing societies and trusts.

To provide mortgage advances.

To exercise powers contained in legislation for improving tenancy relations in private dwelling houses, including the powers to initiate prosecutions for offences.

To exercise powers of management including collection of housing revenue, allocation, sale, letting, maintenance and repair of dwellings vested in the council as a housing authority.

To exercise powers in relation to the employment of directly employed labour.

To assess rents in respect of all council owned housing accommodation and to operate rent rebate schemes in relation thereto, and also the rent allowance schemes for needy private tenants.

To exercise powers of maintenance, repair, letting and management of shops and garages which are vested in the council as a housing authority.

To maintain estate amenities.

To provide a comprehensive housing advisory service.

To exercise all the powers and duties conferred by or under any act, statutory instrument and regulation, on the council as housing authority.[4]

Recent legislation in the United States has moved to increase the role of local government, at least in the planning of federally assisted housing activity. Every metropolitan area is, in effect, required to develop through its areawide planning agency a plan including a specific housing element that "shall take into account all available evidence of the assumptions and statistical bases upon which the projection of zoning, community facilities, and population growth is based, so that the housing needs of both the region and the local communities studied in the plan will be adequately covered in terms of existing and prospective population growth."[5]

The same legislation—the Housing and Community Development Act of 1974—changed the basis of the federally assisted housing program to enlarge the role of the general purpose city government relative to local housing authorities and private builders or landlords. Henceforth the city, as part of its application for a community development block grant (the successor to urban renewal) will have to include a Housing Assistance Plan that is consistent with the housing element of the areawide plan described above and that

a. accurately surveys the condition of the housing stock in the community and assesses the housing assistance needs of lower-income persons (including elderly and handicapped persons, large families, and persons displaced or to be displaced) residing in or expected to reside in the community,
b. specifies a realistic annual goal for the number of dwelling units or persons to be assisted, including (i) the relative proportion of new, rehabilitated, and existing dwelling units, and (ii) the sizes and types of housing projects and assistance best suited to the needs of lower-income persons in the community, and

c. indicates the general locations of proposed housing for lower-income persons, with the objective of (i) furthering the revitalization of the community, including the restoration and rehabilitation of stable neighborhoods to the maximum extent possible, (ii) promoting greater choice of housing opportunities and avoiding undue concentrations of assisted persons in areas containing a high proportion of low-income persons, and (iii) assuring the availability of public facilities and services adequate to serve proposed housing projects.[6]

Developers, and builders, will continue to apply directly to HUD for housing assistance funds rather than to the local government, but HUD in turn must forward the application to the local government, which will determine whether it is consistent with the local housing assistance plan. HUD may still override a local finding that the application is not consistent, but the expectation is that this will happen quite infrequently.

The manner in which these provisions are administered at the federal level is all important and the vigor and sensitivity with which they are pursued remains to be seen. In a sense, they appear to place upon U.S. local government the same sort of responsibility for the planning of publically assisted housing that has traditionally been imposed upon (and accepted) by British local authorities prior to the movement towards a comprehensive housing service. Given the language of the new American legislation, it is possible, although not likely, that the federal government can move local government towards a more comprehensive view of their housing responsibilities than this traditional approach, but such an effort undoubtedly awaits a more activist administration.

Much emphasis, in the United Kingdom, has been put on the operations of housing advice and assistance services, as part of the new comprehensive housing service. Again the Seebohm report's recommendation marked the genesis of this movement (although the existing Catholic Housing Aid Society, a private organization, and the predecessor of Shelter Housing Advice Centre [SHAC] provided the prototype):

It is clear, for instance, that there is a great need for advice and guidance on housing matters.... Advice is needed on the law relating to landlord and tenant, public health requirements, the facilities offered by building societies, the best method of borrowing for house purchase, dangers to be guarded against in buying property and the possibilities of renting in the private market. There is also the urgent need to provide information about rents registered for different sorts of tenancy, rent fixing rights and procedures under the Furnished Houses (Rent Control) Act 1946, and the 1965 Rent Act. In this respect local authorities ought, perhaps, to use more of their power to act for tenants reluctant to use their rights under the 1965 Act. Those with knowledge and resources can usually obtain what advice they need from solicitor, surveyor or bank manager. Many of the people with whom we are concerned, however, cannot easily get advice from these sources, and indeed may present problems which the average professional adviser does not usually meet. A local authority should, we think, provide a centre for housing advice and guidance, to which the public, as well as workers in statutory and voluntary social service agencies, can turn.

Families may be assisted with their housing problems in other ways as well which do not necessarily involve the allocation of a council house. Transfers and exchanges are a good example, ideally including movement between the private and public sectors. A clear liaison should also exist between the work of housing departments and the mortgage loans service operated by most authorities, for, in considering how a family can be helped to acquire decent accommodation, this may be a valuable means. At present local rules of eligibility and conditions of loan sometimes debar families who could be assisted in this way; were they more flexible more people might be helped. Reassurance and advice would also encourage others who would not normally consider applying for a mortgage loan. Likewise local authority loans should be available to less traditional borrowers like tenants' co-operatives, housing associations or self build groups. Such applicants may also need legal aid and technical advice and this should be available, perhaps nationally provided through organisations such as the National Federation of Housing Societies. Local authorities could offer a stepping stone to such further assistance.[7]

The government through both exhortation and financial assistance from its Urban Aid program has encouraged local authorities to establish Housing Aid and Advice Services. According to the Department of Environment's Advisor on Housing Management, the government foresees the centers pursuing the following objectives:

a. to provide greater assistance to individuals by an examination in depth of their housing needs or problems and of the possible methods of meeting them. This can be best achieved by coordinating all sources of housing action and information in one centre. Aid can be given to all who want it, irrespective of their status (e.g., single or student) tenure (e.g., owner-occupier or landlord) or residence (e.g., newcomer or outsider);
b. to discover more information on individual and district housing requirements through a policy of inviting consultation from all people with differing housing needs, and so allow housing policies to be framed to achieve the maximum benefit;
c. to bring about a more rational use of both public and private housing resources.[8]

The first objective relates to servicing the public through any or all of the following means: information (providing clients knowledge of the full range of options and actions available to them); advice (counselling concerning which of the available options he should choose); and action or aid (actual assistance in solving the problem).[9] The second objective is a feedback function that exists as a by-product of the first objective. Through listening to the stream of citizen complaints, questions, and concerns, Housing Aid and Advice Centres ought to be able to provide local housing authorities with a better understanding and knowledge of their citizens' housing needs than was the case in the past. The third objective presumably concerns the use to which local housing authorities will put this feedback.

In short, Housing Aid and Advice Centres are to serve as a combination one stop housing service center and ombudsman for citizens with housing problems or questions. As a social service device they are potentially of enormous importance for they provide the link between an individual's housing problems and the government's professed desire to assure a decent home for every citizen.

Because they are new institutions, Housing Advice Centres (HACs) are still struggling with important questions concerning their form, operations, and relationship to the local housing authority. Should they focus on information, advice, or action, or a combination of these? Given limited resources and an enormous number of inquiries relative to them, upon which portion of their clientele should they concentrate their efforts? Should HACs be a part of the local housing authority structure or should they exist outside of it as an advocate for their client? To what extent should HACs merely attempt to assist their clients within a given housing framework and to what extent should they lobby to change that framework? To what extent should they rely on professionals and to what extent on volunteers? (The highly respected Shelter Housing Aid Centre has relied heavily on volunteers.) Should they be located in areas of housing stress close to their likely clients or in central locations close to local authority housing departments with whom they must work to accomplish their tasks?

At present there are probably 150 Housing Advice Centres, most of which are so new that it is difficult to draw even tentative conclusions from their experience. However, a preliminary report by a Centre for Environmental Studies research team questions the utility of Housing Advice Centres, at least as a means of accomplishing the objectives the HACs posit for themselves. The authors argue that, given the shortage of housing resources and the current system of allocating those resources, Housing Advice Centres can only make changes at the margins within existing priorities. Nor can Housing Advice Centres really perform an independent causal role in bringing about innovation: "information by itself cannot change anything—as we have seen by the spate of Government and local authority reports over the last few years—and where it can change something the local authority would be disposed towards change anyway and information could in most cases be gained by research officers."[10]

The report concludes, paradoxically, that while Housing Advice Centres "have an important role to play both in rationalizing and humanizing bureaucracies," nonetheless they can perform a truly useful function only by failing:

Information which shows that the kind of services an Advice Centre offers only has a limited effect, that despite exploring all the alternatives available to people the situation is getting worse, can only help to strengthen a plea for changes in law and resource allocation. Housing Advice Centres take on a new role of demonstrating that within the confines of present legislation and governmental structures, solutions are short term, difficult or impossible. While not benefitting the worst off directly because they can produce only marginal changes and solutions, ironically Advice Centres can help the poor by being of marginal use to them.[11]

In a sense, the criticism and conclusion is at one and the same time accurate and unfair. It is probably an accurate assessment of what Housing Advice Centres can do, but it may be unfair because it downgrades the importance of rationalizing and humanizing government bureaucracy. Surely the task of creating responsive and humane bureaucracies must rank as one of the most difficult and important problems for modern, industrial states, whether socialist or capitalist, to solve. It is also somewhat unfair, because, while it rightly recognizes the limits for successful action given limited resources and an existing system, it does not appear to pay sufficient attention to the scope for improving peoples' housing conditions even within those constraints. Any housing system, regardless of its resource levels, suffers from imperfect information that reduces the amount of housing services that could be provided below its potential. Presumably, in some situations, the reduction below potential is relatively small and there is little means for improvement within that system—that is, without increasing resources—and in some cases the unused potential might be quite large. One can conceive of Housing Advice Centres as a device for combatting the problem of imperfect information and for helping any housing system, given its present resources, to achieve its full potential.

Within an American context, Housing Advice Centres look particularly attractive for yet another reason. As we have seen, American cities at present play very little role in housing, except for code enforcement. City officials do not accept a housing social service goal as one within their scope of responsibility, nor, apparently, does it occur to citizens that city officials ought to bear such a responsibility, except for code enforcement, environmental services, rodent control, and the limited public housing program. As has been pointed out, this may change to some extent as a result of passage of the Housing and Community Development Act of 1974. Nonetheless, the establishment of Housing Advice Centres would not only perform a humanization and rationalizing (information providing) function in American cities, but would as well provide a city institution or set of institutions that would emphasize the city's potential role and responsibility for dealing with its citizens' housing needs in a more comprehensive fashion either than at present or then the new legislation visualizes. Because it would create a city mechanism concerned with citizen housing problems (even if it only dispensed information), it would, over time, likely bring about a perception on the part of citizens that since the city is the place to take housing problems, it likewise bears some responsibility for solving those problems. Faced with a new demand for services city officials would not only apply more of their own resources towards a housing social service goal, but would themselves attempt to change federal housing policy more towards that end.

Housing and Planning

The United Kingdom has a well-developed planning system that differs from American practice in three important respects: (1) local plans are reviewable by higher levels of government, including ultimately the central government, to ensure coordination and consistency with regional and national policy objectives; (2) local comprehensive plans are legally binding; and (3) detailed land use regulation is not rigidly predetermined through the zoning of areas for specific uses, but is assigned on a case by case basis in response to requests to change existing uses of land (planning permission). Theoretically there exists a flexible means of enforcing national objectives through coordinated local planning policy—a mechanism that does not exist in the U.S.

In the United States, most city governments and metropolitan areas devise "comprehensive" plans but there is no review by a higher level of government to ensure the plans are coordinated and consistent with national or state objectives. The federal government has traditionally played almost no role in local planning decisions;[a] the state governments, which constitutionally have sovereignty in this area, have almost without exception delegated the planning function to their local jurisdictions and retained little or no oversight. As a result, local plans are often uncoordinated and indeed conflicting, which mirrors the opposing political values of different jurisdictions. The major conflict occurs between large cities and the multitude of legally independent suburban jurisdictions that surround them (as well as among the suburban jurisdictions themselves).

More importantly, comprehensive plans in the United States are not legally binding even within the jurisdiction for which they are devised. In theory, the more detailed zoning ordinances are supposed to be based on prior comprehensive plans, but in fact this is seldom the case. And many of the most important infrastructure decisions with respect to sewers, highways, and so forth are taken by semi-independent boards or agencies with little regard for the existing "overall" plan. The plan, in short, is reduced to an exhortation, one of a number of inputs competing to influence the actual shape of development.

---

[a]Although recently it has tried to encourage planning through making federal funds available to cities and metropolitan planning bodies for that purpose—the Section 701 grants—and through requiring local and areawide planning as a precondition to receiving federal grants. Thus a planning mechanism now exists, at least on paper. The federal government is supposed to review local government applications for federal grants to determine whether the use to which these grants will be put is consistent with local and areawide comprehensive plans. (The content of these comprehensive plans is, on the whole, not reviewable by the federal government.) However, while a finding of non-consistency is sufficient to deny the applicant the grant, nonetheless the grant may be approved even if the application is found to be inconsistent with the comprehensive plans. The effectiveness of this process, known as A-95, is thus dependent on the seriousness with which federal agencies administer it, and this has varied substantially from agency to agency. It is also dependent upon the political influence of local mayors with the national administration. Nonetheless most observers feel the A-95 process has enhanced the planning process within metropolitan areas, particularly with respect to bringing about greater coordination of the activities of the multitude of local governments that comprise such an area.

Although structurally the U.K. planning system thus appears a far more potent device for affecting housing policy than does its U.S. counterpart, nonetheless it has been much less effective than might be expected. This results primarily because it has been imposed on a system of local government organization that partially frustrates its intent and causes problems similar in kind, although not in degree to those faced by the United States. Prior to 1974, the planning function was exercised by nearly 200 county boroughs (cities) and counties, each of which drew up strategic structure plans for the approval of central government. City plans were separate from the plans of the surrounding suburban counties. In addition, many of the counties delegated the responsibility for housing plans to smaller district councils.

In April 1974, a new local government system was imposed upon England and Wales (an action which, of course, would be constitutionally impossible in the United States). A two-tiered planning system with less than 100 counties, each of them comprised of several districts, replaced the old system. The counties are to be responsible for developing strategic "structure plans," which must be approved by the central government. Districts will then devise more detailed local plans within the framework of these approved structure plans. However, the structure plans will focus on population, employment, land use, and transport with the primary responsibility for housing located at the district level. The power to grant or withhold planning permission will also be located at the local level.

Placement of the responsibility for housing planning at the local level has in the past greatly diminished the potential for rationality and coordination implicit in the U.K. planning system, and astute observers fear that it will continue to do so.[12] Although local housing plans are reviewable by counties and ultimately by central government, the political realities of enforcing higher level objectives on decision makers representing local communities has lead to a situation not unlike that of central cities and suburbs in the United States. Furthermore, the sheer number of plans and the difficulty in coordinating them has made it almost impossible for central government to play an active, positive role. Instead central government's primary coordinative role has been one of reacting to appeals from individuals, groups, or public bodies who have received adverse decisions in efforts to receive planning permission.

Thus, in neither the United Kingdom nor the United States is it easy to require or persuade localities to build housing when they do not wish to do so or to provide for income or social classes they do not desire to reside in their community. Even the Greater London Council—a metropolitan quasi-government encompassing all 32 London boroughs—has been relatively impotent in this respect. While the individual boroughs have primary housing responsibility, the GLC is invested with certain "overspill" responsibility to provide housing which cuts across borough needs. However, they must first obtain the permission of the borough in whose jurisdiction they wish to provide housing, and the outer (suburban) boroughs have been notably reluctant to grant this. Although central government could overrule the boroughs, it has generally been reluctant to do so.

The fact that plans are legally binding in the United Kingdom, while they are not in the United States, undoubtedly represents a more important difference with respect to housing development. Because the placement of capital infrastructure facilities must be consistent with an overall plan in the United Kingdom, the pattern of residential development (which naturally follows the placement of these facilities) has been controlled and concentrated so that it is consistent with the explicit preferences of British public officials and planners[b] rather than dispersed and sprawling as has occurred in the United States as a result of lack of coherent planning rather than stated preference. As Hall and Clawson observe, the effect of public planning controls has been

... to contain and channel urban growth in Britain in ways that have not been observable in the United States. They have provided greater contiguity of separate residential developments at the local scale, avoiding the leapfrogging and scatteration of subdivisions which have been so characteristic of the United States; but at a larger scale they have deliberately prevented contiguity by restraining the growth of the larger urban areas and channelling development into the smaller towns and villages at some distance away. At the same time they have constantly worked to ensure greater density of development within the residential areas themselves.[13]

The major positive power of British controls results from this internally consistent infrastructure planning. In both the United Kingdom and the United States, the day-by-day implementation of land use controls represents a negative constraint. Planning permission[c] in the United Kingdom or zoning in the United States can prevent undesirable private development from taking place but it cannot *require* desirable private development to occur (although the substantial size of the *public* house building sector in the United Kingdom can mean that an important portion of overall urban development is within the positive control of the local authority).

---

[b]However, there has been much recent debate over the relatively autonomous role planners have played with respect to physical development in the United Kingdom, and serious questions have been asked about the proper relationship of professional experts to citizen preferences within a democratic society.

[c]In 1947, the development rights to all land in the United Kingdom were nationalized. No change in land use of any parcel can occur without receipt of planning permission from the local planning authority. In the United States, zoning is a preset pattern of allowable land use for an area—not for individual plots. However the relative ease of obtaining zoning changes and amendments on individual plots narrows the differences between the two systems.

10 Conclusion

Comparative policy studies, if they are to fulfill our expectations, ought to help stimulate new thinking about policy in both countries. What, if anything, has our examination of housing policy in two different contexts conveyed to us about that policy in each?

Public Sector Housing

Most Americans who look at public sector housing in the United Kingdom are quite impressed and even view it in many cases as a model for the United States to emulate. Indeed, the contrast between public housing in the two countries is striking—and overwhelmingly favorable to the United Kingdom. U.K. council housing is, on the whole, of good quality, well maintained, and not overwhelmed by vandalism and crime. It is on a financially sound basis. It has a socioeconomic mix and is not all bunched together in the poorest or high minority concentration neighborhoods. And it is accepted as legitimate by the vast majority of the British population and most particularly the working class. Each of these attributes stands in striking contrast to public housing in the United States.[a]

However, as many of the above contrasts implicitly suggest, public housing is, in fact, a different animal in the United Kingdom than in the United States—it deals with different problems by different means. It is thus not at all clear how much relevance British public housing has for America's problems. First, U.S. public housing is *not* housing for the working class, which is the way in which U.K. public housing is predominantly perceived. Rather, it is housing primarily for the subworking class—the unemployed, underemployed, single-parent families, and the poverty stricken. It is also, increasingly, housing for blacks.

Many of the usually identified problems of public housing in the U.S. might indeed disappear if it were not, in fact, housing for poor people. This conclusion is a logical one to draw since, to a large extent, public housing's problems are caused by large numbers of poor and deprived households living in high concentrations. Perhaps, as some argue, these problems would be greatly reduced if public housing were not a concentration of poverty-stricken residents, but

---

[a]David Donnison points out that U.K. public sector housing does not differ in these respects from that of most other European countries, such as France, Sweden, Denmark, Holland, Poland, Czechoslovakia and so forth. The point he makes is that it is the United States, rather than the United Kingdom, that is the exception. Communication from David Donnison, Director, Centre for Environmental Studies, London, July 14, 1974.

instead a more extensive mix such as council housing is in the United Kingdom. By scattering the "problem families" and making them a distinct minority in each project, it is argued, the project would be given a chance to succeed, and the "problem families" themselves would improve or be able to be treated as a result of a stable environment.

But what would be the consequences of obtaining such a desirable social mix? Within any given relatively fixed supply of public housing, the result would be that some very poor people who are currently ill-housed in the private rental sector would remain there while substantial numbers of relatively well-off people who could command decent housing on the private market would occupy public sector housing at relatively low rents with high public subsidy. This situation now exists in the United Kingdom where the values of social mix and helping the neediest first are both strongly held. It is a situation that is, quite probably, politically infeasible in the United States for two reasons. First, the rationale for public housing in the public mind clearly is to provide housing for the neediest, for those too poor to obtain decent housing privately, but who nonetheless must be provided shelter. Second, a social mix of the sort that would render the poor and deprived a distinct minority in public housing either implies very few of these types of families would be housed in public housing (in which case public housing would be "successful" but wouldn't be contributing much, if anything, to solving housing problems in the United States) or the size of the public housing sector would have to be both very large indeed and rapidly increasing. And this too is unlikely to happen in the United States.

Partly, it is unlikely to happen because, even if such a social mix would, somehow, be able to make public housing "workable," there would be a nearly insurmountable "how to get from here to there" problem. For given the present state of public housing, both in reality and in perception, very few working-class or middle-class people desire to reside in it. *Perhaps* if the present income and class range in U.S. public housing were similar to that in public housing in the United Kingdom, these groups would be much more interested in occupancy, which would bring about a consequent (so the theory holds) improvement in the conditions of the very poor occupants as well. But the present distribution is not like that in the United Kingdom. Thus, how do you get from here to there?

Furthermore, an important precondition for making public housing a desirable alternative for the working class in the United States is not yet present. Public housing is accepted by the working class in the United Kingdom not only because of different political and social ideologies and traditions, but also because the chronic housing shortage in the United Kingdom and the decline of the private rental sector has limited their housing alternatives and made these alternatives less desirable than public housing. In the United States, however, the private rental sector has served the working and middle classes tolerably well. In addition, owner-occupancy for these groups has been a real and financially feasible alternative to the private rental sector for a much longer period of time in the United States than in the United Kingdom.

To summarize, the housing problem in the United States is largely a problem of housing the lowest portion of the socioeconomic spectrum. It is a problem that is intensifying as that portion of the private rental sector now serving this group continues to decay. The experience of council housing in the United Kingdom does not provide much direction because council housing, although it does represent a considerable social mix, particularly in comparison to the United States, is nonetheless primarily working-class housing, not housing focusing on the most difficult problem families as is true in the United States. It will not do to call for a social-economic mix in U.S. public housing as a means of making public housing work because (1) the preconditions for attaining such a mix do not exist, and (2) unless the public housing program were very large, a social-economic mix would merely mean that public housing was not addressing itself to the most important housing problem facing the United States—the housing of very low-income families.

What *can* the United States learn from British public housing, different beasts though they may be? There are several relatively technical recommendations, all of which seem useful, but none of which will revolutionize the nature of American public housing:

1. Although a real social-economic mix does not seem a realistic possibility, nonetheless it would be desirable to rid public housing of the restrictive features that confine it solely to the poor. First and foremost, the provision requiring present residents to move when their income reaches 125 percent of eligibility level should be removed. Also, the income limits for eligibility, while not being removed, should be increased so that families with income below the median level (instead of below the poverty level as is roughly the case at present) would be eligible.[b]
2. The ability to "pool" gives the British local housing authority a very real financial advantage over the American one. Thus, in the United Kingdom, a local housing authority can apply its revenues and subsidies from all its housing units and estates against their joint cost. In the United States, each project must, in effect, maintain separate finances. Surpluses in one project cannot be used to improve services and eliminate deficits in another. This system should be changed along British lines through creation of a consolidated housing account.
3. The U.S. subsidy system has traditionally been chained to the capital cost of public housing. Recently a limited and insufficient amount of operating subsidy has been made available as a 100 percent grant to hard-pressed local authorities. The United States would do well to adopt the British system of unlimited but *matching* grants for cost increases. The city government should

---

[b]Shortly after the original writing up this recommendation, the Housing and Community Development Act of 1974 did indeed repeal the requirement that residents whose income rose above 125 percent of eligibility levels must move from public housing. Income limits for initial occupancy were also expended, although not as much as is recommended above.

be responsible for the matching, perhaps on a 75-25 percent basis as in the United Kingdom.
4. Housing management is a well-established and honorable profession in the United Kingdom, while it barely exists in the United States in the public sector. Recently a center for housing management has been set up in Washington under federal auspices, which thus represents a first step towards creating a housing management profession. There is no doubt that the development of such a profession with a strong base of expertise would be beneficial; it is doubtful, however, if it could accomplish as much as some of its more ardent proponents sometimes suggest.

The conclusions an American comes to concerning British public housing are inevitably related to the size of the sector. Clearly British council housing represents an impressive feat of public sector mobilization on behalf of the shelter needs of British citizens. Yet council housing is not devoid of serious problems most of which have not been paid very serious attention. These problems relate to the very size and pervasiveness of the sector itself. Perhaps too much effort and energy have been directed towards building large numbers of public housing units and not enough towards some broader questions about peoples' relationship to housing. The questions, which will become more intense with future municipalization of the private rental stock, revolve around the following issues:

1. *Mobility*. The present system of public housing allocation represents a severe impediment to mobility, since it is almost impossible to move directly from one council housing unit in local authority A to another in local authority B without spending a substantial amount of time—sometimes measured in years—on the waiting list.
2. *Choice*. With rare exceptions prospective residents in council housing do not have the option of shopping around and choosing the unit most appropriate to their needs *as they perceive them*. When they come to the top of the list they must choose from a severely constrained number of properties available. Often the ultimate selection is a function of the housing authority's concept of the family's "real need" rather than the family's subjective desires.
3. *Individuality*. A housing unit provides much more than shelter from the elements. It is the secure and protective haven from which human life is sustained. As such, it has an emotional dimension as important, if not more important, as its physical protection dimension. It is a home; not simply a housing unit. Its contours, features, and characteristics are intertwined with an individual's own desires, life styles, and aspirations. A home is thus an extension of an individual's personality. As much scope as possible ought to be allowed for matching an individual with an appropriate housing unit and for shaping that unit to his personality. Large projects or estates consisting of

identical units—or only two or three variations—with limited opportunities for individual decoration, rearrangement, and improvement make this goal very difficult to achieve.

It is not logically impossible for these three goals—mobility, choice and individuality—to exist within the context of public sector housing and a large one at that. But it will take serious thought and a sustained effort at institutional reorganization if this is to be accomplished.

4. *Special Cases.* Council housing in the United Kingdom has served mostly families with children. It has tended to ignore the needs of single individuals, childless couples, students, and transients. These people have, on the whole, been left to fend for themselves in the private rental sector. As this sector continues to decline, what mechanism will arise to meet their needs or will the local housing authority be able to redirect its priorities, even in the face of substantial waiting lists for families with children?
5. *Bureaucracy.* Large bureaucracies by definition are machines for accomplishing stated goals by the application of fixed rules. A concomitant characteristic is that they are inflexible and find it difficult to deal with problems that are not easily handled within the framework of its rules. One of the preeminent problems of modern society—both capitalist and socialist—concerns how to humanize and make responsive these efficient but mechanistic machines. Local housing authorities in the United Kingdom are not immune from this apparently near universal malady of bureaucracies; complaints about their insensitivity, lack of flexibility, and slowness of reaction are common. Yet relatively little has been done to remedy these problems, although the introduction of housing advice centres, partly as a counterforce to housing authorities may be a step in this direction.

The Private Rental Sector

Given the precipitous decline of the private rental sector in the United Kingdom one might think that any lessons for American housing policy would be primarily negative ones. And this is to some extent true. However, there is an important positive lesson as well. The United Kingdom has accepted that shelter is a basic need and that shelter arrangements—including those provided through the private rental sector—should be a primary concern of society. The fact of private ownership does not negate the state's responsibility in this area, but rather may call forth more explicit social service approaches. The United States would do well to accept the spirit of this approach, even if it does not necessarily accept the specific tools the British have applied to implement it.

Neither rent control nor security of tenure in the British style would be desirable or appropriate in the United States. One may seriously question whether they were in the United Kingdom as well. Strict imposition of a rent-control, security-of-tenure policy within the present inner-city context would only hasten the decline of the private rental sector in the United States. And, unlike the United Kingdom, there is no real prospect of a large publicly owned rental sector waiting to take its place. The prospect instead is for worse housing conditions for many people.

Yet this is not so much a rejection of the concept of rent control or security of tenure as a rejection of the British (or New York) method. Something must be done to lower the rental cost *and* improve the quality of lower-income private rental housing. The quality of this housing can be improved—or prevented from deteriorating in the face of lower rent revenues—only in a context that provides the owner of such housing a reasonable return on investment. This clearly will require some form of state subsidy (to meet the owners' needs) and quite probably some form of state control (to assure the tenants' needs are being met). The British have concentrated on the latter to the exclusion of the former.

There are various possible approaches for consideration in the United States. The Section 23 leased housing program in which the city rents standard units at rents providing a reasonable return and then rerents (sublets) the units at subsidized rents to low-income tenants is a good example. It combines a public subsidy with some public control (over structural conditions, maintenance, and so forth) within a context of private ownership. Another possibility is a subsidy to landlords providing they agree to rent at controlled prices (this is similar to the present Section 236 program and is really the functional equivalent of the Section 23 program). Direct housing allowances to tenants have been widely discussed as a means of increasing effective demand, but it is not clear, at least in the short or medium run, how well this approach will work unless it is accompanied by some form of public controls on rents and service standards. In short, there must be some form of subsidy sufficient to allow owners to provide their units with adequate service, maintenance, and repairs and to yield a reasonable return on investment combined with some protection to tenants assuring that the units are, in fact, well-maintained and serviced and that the rents are reasonable. Recent efforts concentrating only on the latter goal such as intensive code enforcement, rent strikes, rent escrow, and receivership programs, although understandable, will likely only worsen the housing situation.

Some form of greater security of tenure also seems long overdue in the United States, but again the British system appears extreme. Instead, it should prove possible to devise a system that provides some balance between the rights of tenants and landlords without at the same time depriving the landlord completely of the right to control his property. Federal legislation could specify that a written lease be mandatory for the letting of all private rental units (except perhaps those specified for transients or in the home of an owner-occupant) and that the lease must conform to certain minimum standards. Thus, for example, it might be desirable to require that all leases be at least one year in length, terminable by the tenant at any time after one month's notice, but requiring a minimum of six month's notice by the landlord prior to rent increases or eviction (except for non-payment of rent or nuisance behavior, both of which would require a court order to evict without the six month's notice). Thus a tenant could terminate his contract at any time after one month's notice, but landlords could change the terms of the contract or evict only at the end of the year's lease and then only if notice had been given at least six months earlier. This system would provide tenants with some degree of security, certainly enough to find new living arrangements in the event of eviction or rent increases they cannot afford. Yet, at the same time, it would retain for the landlord, within some puclicly defined constraints, the ability to use his property as he wishes.

These suggestions may prove workable in the United States, but they would be utterly unrealistic in the United Kingdom given the present state of the private rental sector and the political context within which it exists. That sector appears doomed to continue its decline except for luxury units; the real question concerns what will replace it. The most likely candidate appears to be an enlarged local authority housing sector through acquisition and improvement—or municipalization as this process has been termed. For reasons that have already been discussed in this chapter, a public sector having, in effect, a monopoly on all rental housing poses serious questions with respect to the attainment of other important social goals.

These goals—choice, individuality, mobility, flexibility, and institutional responsiveness—do not exhaust the list of goals societies should and do pursue, nor are they necessarily the most important ones. Furthermore, their attainment in the housing sector would not seem to be logically dependent upon the existence of a rental sector characterized by a substantial degree of private ownership. But it does appear that a private market rental system provides one favorable arrangement for the satisfaction of these values—albeit perhaps at the expense of other important ones—and that the disappearance of that system may, if care is not taken as to its institutional replacement, place these values in jeopardy. If the public sector is to contribute to these social goals, it must undergo substantial reorganization and rethinking as suggested in the previous section. A substantial quasi-public third force consisting of housing associations, cooperatives, and co-ownership schemes might be desirable both as a means of assuring some choice, individuality, and mobility and as a means of prodding the public sector to greater responsiveness.

Owner-occupancy

The greatest similarity between the two countries in the area of housing policy lies in the owner-occupancy sector. Both countries have encouraged home ownership through favorable tax treatment. This policy, when added to the apparent strong preference for homeownership on the part of much of the citizenry, has resulted in a majority of households in each of the countries owning their own home.

Both countries have also made modest efforts to extend the opportunity for homeownership to low-income families. The United States has utilized a deep subsidy for a small number of low-income families, while the United Kingdom has opted for a shallow subsidy (the option mortgage) available to all low-income purchasers.

Although the soaring price of houses and mortgage interest rates has frustrated the option mortgage as a device for making homeownership a viable choice for the majority of low-income households, nonetheless the rationale for this approach seems particularly potent on equity grounds. Deductions of mortgage interest from taxable income in graduated tax systems are regressive in the classic sense, for they provide proportionately more benefit to those who have higher income than to those who have lower income and they provide no benefit at all to those whose income is so low that there is no tax on it. The option mortgage provides those families having incomes below the tax threshold with a government subsidy roughly equivalent to the tax savings they would receive from their interest deductions if they were paying the standard rate of tax—the rate paid by the great majority of U.K. taxpayers.

The United States would do well to adopt a similar approach, although the difference in the tax systems would make the program somewhat more complex. In the United Kingdom, most households with income above the tax threshold pay a single standard rate with a surtax being charged on the highest incomes. In the United States, there are many small incremental increases in marginal tax rates as income rises. Thus an option mortgage scheme might have to provide government subsidies equal to the relief provided to a taxpayer paying at the average tax rate paid by all taxpayers.

For its part, the United Kingdom perhaps could look carefully at U.S. mortgage market institutions. The U.S. system of mortgage insurance has made mortgages more readily available to families that might otherwise be considered too "risky" and has made them available on easy terms. The secondary mortgage market institutions described in Chapter 7, while having by no means solved the problem of how to maintain a steady flow of mortgage funds, have achieved at least a modicum of success and appear to suggest the possibility of approaches less extreme than the variable interest rate and high interest rates in general.

The Role of Local Government

Throughout this study we have emphasized the different roles played by local government with respect to housing in the two countries. In the United

Kingdom, municipalities have primary responsibility for housing, which on the whole is viewed by them in social service terms. In the United States, most municipalities assume little responsibility for the housing situation of their citizens; it is not perceived as a routine function of local government and certainly not in social service terms.

However, housing is a function for which, at least on a day-to-day administrative basis, the local government must accept responsibility if a social service approach is to be pursued at all. If such an approach is desirable—and however unimplemented it may be, it is enshrined in the preamble to the Housing Act of 1949—then a way must be designed to encourage greater local government activity in and responsibility for housing. How can this be done?

At present, most housing programs are operated by the federal government through subsidies either to quasi-autonomous local housing authorities (public housing) or through subsidies to private entities (builders, investors, home buyers, and so forth). Given the fiscal difficulties of U.S. city governments and the high cost of meeting housing needs, local governments clearly would require substantial federal resources even if they did wish to initiate major housing activities, but at present federal housing subsidies offer little scope for local government participation.

These programs should be reshaped into a single, block housing grant that flows directly to city governments. The legislation might specify the categories for which the money could be used but leave the exact division of the funds up to the locality (subject to federal government approval); preferably, a substantial portion of the funds should be available for innovative use by the locality. The funds should only be granted upon the federal government's approval of a five-year housing need plan and an annual housing action plan submitted by the local government. The action plan should detail how the year's funds would be applied to meeting the area's housing needs with a mandatory provision that those with the greatest housing needs (it would be preferable to use this phrase rather than "low-income families") should be given top priority. The housing plan should have to be consistent with the required housing element of the metropolitan-wide comprehensive plan as determined by the metropolitan-wide planning agency receiving federal planning funds.[c] And it should have to meet strong anti-discrimination criteria.

It would be preferable, in fact, if the entire grant were to go to some metropolitan agency with powers to allocate the funds to the various jurisdictions according to the metropolitan area's need and with the residual power to build or provide housing anywhere within a jurisdiction if that jurisdiction proves recalcitrant. However preferable this may be, it does not appear even remotely politically feasible. Perhaps a strong incentive could be established by

---

[c]The Housing and Community Development Act of 1974, signed into law in August by President Ford, moved somewhat towards meeting the recommendations set forth in this paragraph. See pp. 97-98.

providing an additional grant—say 25 percent higher—for each participating jurisdiction if the entire program were run through a metropolitan agency.

The federal government through the Federal Housing Administration (FHA) or some successor organization would continue to act as a mortgage insurance agency for individual houses including those funded through the block grant. However, FHA's criteria for approving mortgage loans should be changed to explicitly include consumer-oriented criteria protecting the purchaser or tenant as well as economic risk criteria protecting the lender. Thus mortgages might be approved only for units meeting acceptable structural and use standards and only if certain minimum contract or lease provisions are adhered to.

Finally, recipient jurisdictions should be required to establish housing advice and assistance centers and provided with federal funds for this purpose. The centers would be separate from the city housing department and, while agencies of the city government, would function in an ombudsman and semi-advocacy fashion. They could be expected to be, in addition, the focal point for bringing the expression of citizen housing needs to the attention of city officials.

By providing local governments with the resources for helping to meet their citizens' housing needs, and by establishing a mechanism for expression of those needs and an expectation that the city ought to meet them, city governments can be both encouraged—and coerced by their voters—to accept responsibility for implementing a housing social service approach. It is likely that most cities would be politically unable to ignore the offer of substantial federal resource inputs even if accompanied by a degree of federal control over the use of those resources. However, if non-acceptance were thought to be potentially a serious problem, it could be discouraged through a penalty such as the loss of 25 percent of revenue-sharing funds for cities refusing to participate.

Conclusion

Our examination of housing policy in the United States and United Kingdom has led us less to recommendations that elements of one country's policy be transferred to the other than to new ways of looking at each country's housing problems, policies, and programs. These changed perceptions and perspectives do not necessarily result in the conclusion that a particular approach is superior or ought to be transferred from one country to the other, although we have not hesitated to make such judgements or suggestions when appropriate. Rather they provoke new thinking about a variety of different alternatives and options. The test of the value of such an endeavor must ultimately lie in whether public policy itself changes in response to these new ways of defining problems and to a broadening of the scope of alternatives.

Notes

Notes

Chapter 1
The Context of Housing Policy

1. Anthony Downs, "The Successes and Failures of Federal Housing Policies," *The Public Interest*, No. 34, Winter 1974, p. 142. Copyright © 1974 by National Affairs, Inc.
2. Louis S. Rosenburg, "New Perspectives on Housing Need: A Case Study of the Low-Income Housing Problem in Baltimore, Maryland," unpublished Ph.D. dissertation. Department of City and Regional Planning, University of Pennsylvania, 1973, pp. 213-21.
3. Valerie A. Karn, *Housing Standards and Costs: A Comparison of British Standards and Costs with Those in the U.S.A., Canada and Europe* (Birmingham: Center for Urban and Regional Studies, University of Birmingham, 1973), pp. 24-27.
4. U.S., President of the United States, *Fourth Annual Report on National Housing Goals*, GPO, p. 37; U.K., Department of Environment, *House Condition Survey 1971, England and Wales*, HMSO, p. 13.
5. Data from U.K., Department of Environment, *Housing and Construction Statistics*, HMSO, No. 7, 1973, and No. 3, 1972; U.K., Central Statistical Office, *Social Trends*, HMSO, No. 4, 1973, p. 156; David Birch, et al., Joint Center for Urban Studies, *America's Housing Needs*, Cambridge, Mass., 1973, p. 3-18.

Chapter 2
Housing as a Social Service

1. T.H. Marshall, *Social Policy* (London: Hutchinson University Library, 1970), p. 166.
2. U.K., *Widening the Choice: The Next Step in Housing*, HMSO, Cmnd. 5280, April 1973, pp. 11-12.
3. Anthony Crosland, "Towards a Labour Housing Policy," *Fabian Tract 410* (London: Fabian Society, July 1971), pp. 5-6.
4. David Donnison, "Towards a Comprehensive Housing Service," Conference of English Housing Authorities, October 1971, p. 17.
5. John T. Macey and Charles Vivien Baker, *Housing Management* (London: The Estates Gazett Ltd, 2nd Ed., 1973), p. 37.
6. John Macey, *Publically Provided and Assisted Housing in the U.S.A.* (Washington, D.C.: Urban Institute, 1972), p. 25.
7. U.S., Bureau of the Census, *Statistical Abstract of the United States, 1972* GPO, 1972, p. 410.

8. U.K., Central Statistical Office, *Social Trends*, HMSO, No. 4, 1973, p. 187.

Chapter 3
Public Housing

1. U.K., Central Statistical Office, *Social Trends*, HMSO, No. 4, 1973, p. 156.
2. U.K., Department of Environment, *Housing and Construction Statistics*, HMSO, No. 7, 3rd Quarter, 1973, p. 20.
3. U.K., Ministry of Housing and Local Government, *Old Houses into New Homes*, HMSO, Cmnd. 3602, 1968, p. 1.
4. Trevor Roberts, *A Review of Recent Developments in Housing Policy* (Liverpool: Liverpool Polytechnic Department of Town and County Planning, 1973).
5. U.S., Department of Housing and Urban Development, *Housing in the 1970s* (Washington, D.C.: HUD, 1973), p. 4-81.
6. Anthony Crosland, "Towards a Labour Housing Policy," *Fabian Tract 410* (London: Fabian Society, 1971), pp. 11-12.
7. Henry J. Aaron, *Shelter and Subsidies: Who Benefits from Federal Housing Policies* (Washington, D.C.: Brookings Institution, 1972), p. 117.
8. Irving Welfeld, "That Housing Problem," *The Public Interest*, No. 27, Spring 1972, p. 89. Copyright © 1972 by National Affairs, Inc.
9. U.K., Department of Environment, *Housing Associations*, HMSO, 1971, p. 119.
10. U.K., Central Statistical Office, *Social Trends*, HMSO, No. 4, 1973, p. 158.
11. U.K., Department of Environment, *Widening the Choice: The Next Steps in Housing*, HMSO, Cmnd. 5280, April 1973, pp. 10-11.
12. U.K., *Hansard*, House of Commons, Vol. 873, No. 33, 6 May 1974, p. 48.

Chapter 4
Private Rental Housing

1. J.B. Cullingworth, *Housing and Local Government* (London: George Allen and Unwin, 1966), p. 25.
2. U.K., Central Statistical Office, *Social Trends*, HMSO, No. 4, 1973, p. 162.
3. Adella A. Nevitt *The Nature of Rent Control Legislation in the U.K.*, Centre for Environmental Studies, University Working Paper No. 8, London, 1970, pp. 21-22.

4. U.K., *Report of the Committee on the Rent Acts*, HMSO, Cmnd. 4609, 1971, pp. 82-83.

5. Ibid., p. 80.

6. Ibid., p. 83.

7. Ira S. Lowry, Joseph S. De Salvo, and Barbara Woodfell, *Rental Housing in New York City, Vol. II, The Demand for Shelter* (New York: Rand Institute, 1971), p. 102.

8. Ibid., p. 90.

9. U.K., *Report of the Committee on the Rent Acts*, HMSO, Cmnd. 4609, 1971, p. 62.

10. Ira Lowry, ed., *Rental Housing in New York City, Vol. I, Confronting the Crisis* (New York: Rand Corp., 1971), p. 12.

11. Adella A. Nevitt, *Housing, Taxation and Subsidies* (London: Thomas Nelson and Sons, 1966), p. 43.

12. Ibid., p. 42.

13. Paul Taubman and Robert Rasche, "Subsidies, Tax Law and Real Estate Investment," in U.S., Congress, Joint Economic Committee, *The Economics of Federal Subsidy Programs, Part 3–Tax Subsidies*, GPO, 1972, p. 343.

14. Henry Aaron, *Shelter and Subsidies: Who Benefits from Federal Housing Policies* (Washington, D.C.: Brookings Institution, 1972), p. 54.

15. U.K., Department of Environment, *Housing and Construction Statistics*, HMSO, 1st Quarter, 1972, Table 3.

16. Ibid., Table 11.

17. Ibid., Table 3.

18. U.K., Department of Environment, *Housing and Construction Statistics*, HMSO, 2nd Quarter, 1973, No. 6, p. 90.

19. Alex Henney, *London's Housing Situation*, mimeo, April 1974, Exhibit 2.

20. U.K., *Report of the Committee on the Rent Acts*, Cmnd. 4609, 1971, pp. 130-31.

21. U.S., Department of Housing and Urban Development, *Housing in the Seventies* (Washington, D.C.: HUD, 1973), p. 6-7.

22. U.S., Bureau of Census, *Statistical Abstract of the U.S. 1972*, GPO, 1972, p. 683.

23. U.S., Senate, Statement of Neil Hardy, Assistant Administrator Housing and Development Administration, New York City before Senate, Committee on Banking and Currency 91-92, *Housing and Urban Legislation of the 1970s*, p. 807.

24. Michael Stegman, *Housing Investment in the Inner City: The Dynamics of Decline* (Cambridge, Mass.: MIT Press, 1972), p. 260.

25. David Birch et al., *America's Housing Needs: 1970 to 1980* (Cambridge, Mass.: Joint Center for Urban Studies, December 1973), p. 4-11.

26. U.K., *Report of the Committee on Local Authority and Allied Social Services*, HMSO, Cmnd. 3703, 1968, p. 124.

27. U.K., Department of Environment, *House Condition Survey 1971, England and Wales*, House Survey Reports, No. 9, HMSO, 1971, Table 18.

28. Malcolm Wicks, "Rented Housing and Social Ownership," *Fabian Tract 421* (London: Fabian Society, 1973), p. 19.

29. Society of Labour Lawyers, *The End of the Private Landlord*, Fabian Research Series, No. 312 (London: Fabian Society, September 1973), p. 3.

30. Ibid., p. 15.

31. U.K., Department of Environment, *Local Authority Housing Programmes*, HMSO, Circular 70/74, April 19, 1974, p. 28.

32. Ibid., p. 30.

33. George Sternlieb, "Abandonment and Rehabilitation: What is to be Done?" in U.S., Congress, House of Representatives, Committee on Banking and Currency, *Papers submitted to Subcommittee on Housing Panels*, Vol. 1, GPO, 1971, pp. 325-6.

Chapter 5
Security of Tenure

1. Adella Nevitt, *Nature of Rent Control Legislation in the U.K.*, Centre for Environmental Studies, University Working Paper No. 8, London, 1970, pp. 22-23.

2. Phillip Pearson, *A New Deal for Furnished Tenants* (London: Shelter, 1974), p. 3.

3. Louis Rosenburg, "New Prospectives on Housing Need: A Case Study of the Low-Income Housing Problem in Baltimore, Maryland," unpublished Ph.D. dissertation (Department of City and Regional Planning, University of Pennsylvania, 1973), pp. 255-64.

4. *Boston Housing Authority v Ruth Hemingway*, 293 NE 2nd 831, p. 842.

5. "Developments in Contemporary Landlord-Tenant Relations: An Annotative Bibliography," *Vanderbilt Law Review*, May 1973, pp. 727-8, 740.

6. Ibid.

7. Thomas M. Quinn and Earl Phillips, "The Law of Landlord-Tenant: A Critical Evaluation of the Past with Guidelines for the Future," *Fordham Law Review* 38, p. 229.

8. Michael Stegman, *Housing Investment in the Inner City* (Cambridge, Mass.: MIT Press, 1972), pp. 73-74.

9. George Sternlieb, "Abandonment and Rehabilitation" in U.S., House of Representatives, Committee on Banking and Currency, *Papers submitted to Sub-Committee on Housing Panels*, Part 1, GPO, 1971, pp. 316-7.

Chapter 6
Rent Subsidies and Allowances

1. U.S., Department of Housing and Urban Development, *Housing for the Seventies* (Washington, D.C.: HUD, 1973), pp. 2-25, 2-26.

Chapter 7
Homeownership

1. U.S., Department of Housing and Urban Development, *Housing in the Seventies* (Washington, D.C.: HUD, 1973), p. 8-10.
2. Data derived from HUD; Ibid., ch. 8.
3. U.K., Department of Environment, *Housing and Construction Statistics*, HMSO, No. 7, 3rd Quarter, 1973, p. 2.
4. U.K., Department of Environment, *Housing and Construction Statistics*, HMSO, No. 8, 4th Quarter, 1973, p. 45.
5. U.K., Central Statistical Office, *Social Trends*, HMSO, No. 4, 1973, p. 163.
6. U.S., Department of Housing and Urban Development, *Housing in the Seventies* (Washington, D.C.: HUD, 1973), ch. 3.
7. Henry Aaron, *Shelter and Subsidies: Who Benefits from Federal Housing Policies* (Washington, D.C.: Brookings Institution, 1972), p. 77.

Chapter 8
Maintenance of Housing Stock

1. Daniel Mandelker, "Strategies in English Slum Clearance and Housing Policies," *U. of Wisconsin Law Review*, 1969, p. 806.
2. John Macey and Charles Baker, *Housing Management* (London: Estates Gazette Ltd., 2nd Ed.), 1973, pp. 190-1.
3. U.S., National Commission on Urban Problems, *Building the American City*, GPO, 1968, p. 276.
4. Ibid., p. 276.
5. Ibid., p. 286.
6. Michael Stegman, *Housing Investment in the Inner City* (Cambridge, Mass.: MIT Press, 1972), pp. 262-3.
7. William Grigsby, "Economic Aspects of Code Enforcement," *Urban Lawyer*, Fall 1971, p. 536. Reprinted by permission from 3 *Urban Lawyer* 536 (Fall 1971), published by the American Bar Association, Section on Local Government Law.
8. U.K., Ministry of Housing and Local Government, *Old Houses into New Homes*, HMSO, Cmnd. 3602, April 1968, p. 1.
9. U.K., Central Statistical Office, *Social Trends*, HMSO, No. 4, 1973, p. 158.
10. Ibid.
11. U.K., *Better Homes: The Next Priorities*, HMSO, Cmnd. 5339, June 1973, pp. 11-12.
12. Michael Stegman, *Housing Investment in the Inner City* (Cambridge, Mass.: MIT Press, 1972), p. 227.

13. Henry J. Aaron, *Shelter and Subsidies* (Washington, D.C.: Brookings Institution, 1972), p. 183.

Chapter 9
The Role of Local Government

1. U.K., *Report of the Committee on Local Authority and Allied Personal Social Services*, HMSO, Cmnd. 3703, 1968, p. 124.
2. J.B. Cullingworth, *Problems of Urban Society*, Vol. II (London: Allen and Unwin, 1973), p. 55.
3. The Institute of Housing Managers, *The Comprehensive Housing Services—Organization and Functions* (London: Institute of Housing Managers, June 1972), p. 1.
4. Ibid., p. 5.
5. U.S., House of Representatives, "Housing and Community Development Act of 1974 Conference Report," Report No. 93-1279, 93rd Congress, 2nd Session, p. 61.
6. Ibid., p. 6.
7. U.K., *Report of the Committee on Local Authority and Allied Personal Social Services*, HMSO, Cmnd. 3703, 1968, p. 124.
8. Derek Fox, *Housing Aid and Advice*, U.K., Department of Environment, HMSO, 1973, mimeo, p. 10.
9. Paul Byrne, "Housing Aid," *New Society*, September 2 1971, p. 415.
10. Michael Harloe, Richard Minns, Jennifer Stoker, "Who Needs Housing Advice Centers" (London: Centre for Environmental Studies, 1973), mimeo, p. 3.
11. Ibid., pp. 3-4.
12. Conversation with Robin Thompson, Structure Planning team, Centre for Environmental Studies.
13. Marion Clawson and Peter Hall, *Planning and Urban Growth: An Anglo-American Comparison* (Baltimore: Johns Hopkins University Press, 1973), p. 136.

Index

Aaron, Henry, 50
Ashley, Thomas Rep., 75

Birch, David, et al., 54n
Briggs, B. Bruce, 75n
Building societies (U.K.), 79, 81

Centre for Environmental Studies, 100
Comprehensive housing service (U.K.), 17, 96-97
Condominia (U.S.), 47-48, 64n
Conservative Party (Government): attitude towards Housing Associations and Societies, 39; attitude towards security of tenure, 62; attitude towards size of public housing sector, 21; lack of support for GLC overspill powers, 36; proposal to release Green Belt land for housing, 78; public sector starts during government, 22; support of mortgage market institutions, 81; view of housing as a social service, 16-17
Cost yardstick (U.K.), 23
Council housing. *See* Public housing
Crosland, Anthony, 16, 30, 39, 76
Cullingworth, J.B., 42, 95-96

DeLeeuw, Frank, 35n
Department of Environment (U.K.), 23, 55n
Department of Housing and Urban Development (HUD [U.S.]), 37, 45, 72, 98
Donnison, David, 17, 105n
Downs, Anthony, 9, 18n

Fair rent (U.K.), 27-30, 43-44, 68, 69; defined, 43-44; experience under, 43; Labour Party attitude towards, 43
Federal Home Loan Bank Board (U.S.), 81
Federal Home Loan Mortgage Corporation (U.S.), 81
Federal Housing Administration (FHA) insured mortgage loan (U.S.), 24n, 37, 80n, 81-82, 93, 114
Federal National Mortgage Association, 81
Federally assisted privately owned housing, U.S., 36-38, 98 (*see also* public housing); advantages and disadvantages compared to public housing, 37-38; rent subsidy mechanism in, 68; rent supplement, 68; section 23, 26, 35, 110; section 235 (homeownership), 24n, 37, 80; section 236 (rental), 24n, 37, 70, 110
Fordham Law Review, 66
Francis Committee (U.K.), 44, 46, 51, 63n
Furnished Tenancies (U.K.), 44, 61n, 63, 91

Government National Mortgage Association, (U.S.), 81
Greater London Council: municipalization program, 58; overspill powers, 36, 103
Grigsby, William, 89

Homeownership, 75-83;
– consumer protection, 82-83
– homeownership costs, 78-79
– house prices, increase in, U.S. and U.K., 75-78; causes of, 77-78
– mortgage costs, 79-82
– recommendations for U.K., 112
– recommendations for U.S., 112
– similarities, U.S. and U.K., 111-112
Housing Act of 1949 (U.K.), 90
Housing Act of 1949 (U.S.), 18
Housing Act of 1968 (U.S.), 24
Housing Advice Centres (U.K.), 98-101; evaluation of, 100-101; objectives of, 99-100; recommendation for U.S. adoption, 101, 114
Housing and Community Development Act of 1974 (U.S.), 26, 33n, 60n, 81n, 87n, 97-98, 101, 107n, 113
Housing allowance (U.S.), 72-73, 110
Housing Associations and Societies (U.K.), 38-39, 111
Housing codes (unfit housing, U.K.), 85-90
– categories regulated, 87; development of, 87-88; economic consequences of, 88-89; Federally Assisted Code Enforcement Program (FACE), 88; problems with enforcement, 88; workable program, 87-88
– U.K., 85-86; occupancy standards, 87n; standard of fitness, 86
– U.S., 87-90
Housing condition and quality of stock, U.K., 9, 10; U.S., 10
Housing Corporation (U.K.), 38
Housing Finance Act of 1972 (U.K.), 27-30, 29n, 38, 43, 68, 69
Housing investment, 10-11, 18-19, 23; expenditure as a percent of national budget, 18-19
Housing revenue account (U.K.), 26-27, 71

Improvement grants (U.K.), 23, 90-92. *See also* Rehabilitation (U.S.)
Institute of Housing Managers (U.K.), 55, 96

Joint Center for Urban Studies (Harvard-MIT), 54

Labour Party (Government): approach to municipalization by 1974 Government, 57-58; attitude towards Housing Association and Societies, 39; attitude towards security of tenure, 62, 91; attitude towards size of public housing sector, 21; imposition of rent freeze in 1974, 55; proposal for nationalization of land in path of development, 78; public sector starts during Government, 22, reaction to Fair Rents, 29, 30; support of mortgage market institutions, 81; support of municipalization, 55; view of housing as a social service, 16-17
Landlord-tenant law; development and basis of, 61; recommendation for reform, 110-111
Leeman, Sam, 35n
Local government (local authority, U.K.): decision to build public sector housing, U.K., 22-23; degree of responsibility for housing policy, U.K., 6, 17-18, 55, 95-96; degree and responsibility for housing policy, U.S., 6, 17-18, 37, 97-98, 101, 113; financial contribution towards public housing, U.K., 26; financial contribution towards public housing, U.S., 27-28, 30; recommendation and proposal for increased responsibility for housing policy, U.S., 113-114; relationship to national government, 5-6
Lowry, Ira, et al., 46n

Macey, John, 18
Marshall, T.H., 15
Mortgages: and tax law, 79; insured mortgages (U.S.), 81-82 (see also FHA); mortgage institutions, U.K., 79, 112; mortgage institutions, U.S., 81-82, 112; option mortgage (U.K.), 79-80; subsidized mortgage (U.S.), 80; variable interest rate (U.K.), 80-81
Morton, Jane, 7n
Municipalization, 55-58; by default (U.S.), 58; Labour Government circular on, 57-58

National Association of Homebuilders (NAHB [U.S.]), 83
National Commission on Urban Problems (U.S.), 87, 88
National Housebuilders Registration Council (NHBRC [U.K.]), 82-83
Nevitt, Della, 44, 62
Nixon, President Richard; economic stabilization policy and rent control, 42; suspends housing programs, 26, 29, 72, 80

Occupancy Standards (U.K.), 87n
Option mortgage (U.K.), 79-80, 112

Planning System, 102-104
—A-95 process, 102n; comprehensive planning program (Section 701), 102; lack of coordination, 102; zoning, 104
—comparison, U.S. and U.K., 102-104
—relationship to housing, U.S., U.K., 103-104
—U.K., 103-104; nationalization of development rights, 104n; planning permission, 104; responsibility for housing planning, 103; structure plans, 103
—U.S., 102
Private rental sector, 41-60
—rent level as percent of income in U.S. and U.K., 52
—size of in U.S. and U.K., 47-48
—tax and subsidy policy towards, in U.S. and U.K., 48-50
—U.K.: inadequate economic return on, 51; physical condition of stock, 50-51; proposals for municipalization of stock, 55-58; reasons for decline of, 48-49; recommendations for, 111; security of tenure in, 62-63
—U.S.: abandonment in inner-city, 53; deterioration of inner-city market, 53-54; increase in rent burden on tenant, 54; municipalization by default, 58; remedies for problems of, 58-60
Public housing (Council housing), 21-40
—contrasts, U.S., U.K., 105-107
—finance, 26-31; operating cost subsidy, U.S., 30; revenues, composition of, U.K., 27; revenues, composition of, U.S., 28; subsidy systems, U.K., 27, 30; subsidy systems, U.S., 28-30
—location, 35-36
—opposition to placement in neighborhoods, 35-36
—problems with, in U.K., 108-109
—recommendations for U.S., 107-108
—rent, U.K., 28, 67
—rent, U.S., 67
—size and scope of public sector, U.K., 21-24
—size and scope of public sector, U.S., 24-25
—starts in U.K., Conservative and Labour Governments compared, 22-24
—starts in U.S., Republican and Democratic Administrations compared, 25-26
—tenants, 31-35; eligibility, U.K., 31; eligibility, U.S., 32-33; mobility, U.K., 36; selection, U.K., 31; socioeconomic com-

position of, U.K., 32, 34; socioeconomic composition of, U.S., 33-35
Public Works Loan Board (U.K.), 79

Rand Institute, study of rental housing in New York, 45, 46
Rasche, Robert, 49
Rehabilitation (U.S.), 92-93. *See also* Improvement grants (U.K.)
Rent Act of 1957 (U.K.), 43, 68
Rent Act of 1965 (U.K.), 43, 63
Rent
—income ratio, 11, 52
—U.K.: public housing, 28-29, 67; private sector, 52
—U.S.: public housing, 67; private sector, 52
Rent control, 41-47, 73, 109-110
—New York City, 42, 45, 46
—U.K., 42-47, 109-110; economic consequences of, 44, 46-47, 110; furnished tenancies not subject to, 44; history of, 42-43; impact on housing, 46; impact on unfurnished tenancies, 44-45; relationship to security of tenure, 61-62
—U.S., 42, 45; impact in New York City, 46-47; on federally assisted housing programs, 45
Rent Scrutiny Board, 29
Rent subsidy schemes
—U.K., 67, 68; criticism of, 68-70; financing of, 70-71; supplementary benefits, 71
—U.S., 68, 70; Housing Allowance, 72-73; public assistance, 72
Rent Tribunal (U.K.), 44, 63
Roberts, Trevor, 23
Romney, George, 9
Rosenburg, Louis, 9, 64

Security of tenure, 61-66
—U.K.: economic consequences of, 63, 109-110; extended to furnished tenancies, 91; harassment, penalty for, 63; relationship to rent control, 61-62
—U.S.: lack of security of tenure, 63-66; prohibition of retaliatory eviction, 64; recommendations for U.S., 110-111
Seebohm Committee (U.K.), 55, 95, 98
Shelter Housing Advice Centre (SHAC), 63, 98
Social Service approach to housing: defined, 16; effect of rent control as, 45-46; homeownership as, 75; housing allowance as, 72-73; rent subsidies as, 67; security of tenure as, 62; in U.K., 16-18, 20, 41-42, 55, 95-96, 109; in U.S., 18-19, 20
Social Service philosophy, 15
Society of Labour Lawyers, 56, 57
Squatting, 51n
Stafford, David, 27n
Stegman, Michael, 53, 66, 89
Sternlieb, George, 58, 66
Supplementary benefits (U.K.), 71, 72n

Taubman, Paul, 49
Tenure, 12-13, 47-48, 75
Titmus, Richard, 3n

Unfit housing. *See* Housing codes
United Kingdom
—economic tradition, 4
—Housing policy, 7-9; historical developments of, 7; perception of housing problem, 8-9; political cleavage surrounding, 7
—ideology, 3
—local finance, 6
—political structure, 5
—social philosophy, 4
—wealth, 10-11
United States
—economic tradition, 14
—housing policy, 7-9; historical development, 7; perception of housing problem, 8-9; political cleavage surrounding, 7
—ideology, 3
—local finance, 4
—political structure, 5
—social philosophy, 4
—wealth, 1-11
Urban renewal (U.S.), 87n

Vanderbilt Law Review, 65

Warrant of Habitability (U.S.), 65-66
White Papers: "Widening the Choice: The Next Step in Housing," 16, 39; "Better Homes: The Next Priority," 92
Wicks, Malcolm, 56
Wilmot, Peter, 69n

About the Author

Harold L. Wolman, associate professor of politics at the University of Massachusetts-Boston, received the Ph.D. in political science from the University of Michigan in 1968. During 1973-74, he was the recipient of a National Endowment for the Humanities Fellowship and was a visiting fellow at the Centre for Environmental Studies in London. Professor Wolman has also been a legislative assistant to Sen. Adlai E. Stevenson of Illinois (1971-1973) and, prior to that, Associate Director of the National Priorities Project at the National Urban Coalition. He is the author of *Politics of Federal Housing* and coeditor of *Counterbudget*.